WHAT'S WRONG

WITH UNIVERSITY

WHAT'S WRONG WITH UNIVERSITY

and how to make it work for you anyway

JEFF RYBAK

ECW Press

Published by ECW PRESS
2120 Queen Street East, Suite 200, Toronto, Ontario, Canada M4E 1E2

LIBRARY AND ARCHIVES OF CANADA CATALOGUING IN PUBLICATION

Rybak, Jeff
What's wrong with university: and how to make it work for you anyway / Jeff Rybak.

Includes bibliographical references.

ISBN-13: 978-1-55022-776-5
ISBN-10: 1-55022-776-9

1. College student orientation—Canada. 2. Education, Higher—Aims and objectives—Canada. 3. Universities and colleges—Canada. i. Title.

LB2343.3.R92 2007   378.1'980971   C2006-906800-3

Interior and back cover illustrations: Evan Munday
Cover photo: A. Huber/U. Starke/Corbis
Author photo: Kevin Wong
Editor: Emily Schultz
Development and typesetting: David Caron
PRINTED AND BOUND IN CANADA: Webcom

This book is set in Sabon, designed by Jan Tschichold in 1964. The chapter headings are in Sackers Gothic, created by the Monotype Design Studio. The sub-headings are in Franklin Gothic, designed by Morris Fuller Benton in 1902, and redrawn by Victor Caruso in 1980. The book is printed on Legacy TB Natural, from 100% post-consumer-waste recycled pulp.

The publication of *What's Wrong With University* has been generously supported by the Canada Council for the Arts which last year invested $20.1 million in writing and publishing throughout Canada, by the Ontario Arts Council, by the Government of Ontario through Ontario Book Publishing Tax Credit, and the Government of Canada through the Book Publishing Industry Development Program (BPIDP).

Canada   Canada Council   Conseil des Arts
          for the Arts   du Canada

DISTRIBUTION
CANADA: Jaguar Book Group, 100 Armstrong Avenue,
Georgetown, Ontario, L7G 5S4
UNITED STATES: IPG, 814 North Franklin Street,
Chicago, Illinois 60610

First printing, 2007

ECW PRESS
ecwpress.com

TABLE OF CONTENTS

INTRODUCTION IX

CHAPTER ONE
THE FUNCTIONS OF EDUCATION I
What Happens in a School I
Why Go to University? I I

CHAPTER TWO
THE MODERN UNIVERSITY 23
How Does It Happen? 23
How Does it Get Measured? 34
What Do You Get? 43
When Things Go Wrong 49
What Comes Next? 65

CHAPTER THREE
GETTING MORE OF WHAT *YOU* WANT 75
What You Can't Control 75
The Academic Student 79
The Vocational Student 95
The Certification Student I06
The Good Citizen I I 2
The Holding-Pen Student I26

CHAPTER FOUR

INTERNAL CONTRADICTIONS 135

Things That Don't Make Sense 135

Grading 136

Too Cool for School 147

Competing Agendas and Politicization 154

Private or Public, Consumer or User? 160

Eroding Value and Graduating "Everyone" 169

Why Does It Hang Together? 177

CHAPTER FIVE

THE BIG PICTURE 183

Beyond the Personal 183

The Universality of University 184

The Scam 195

Further 205

CHAPTER SIX

THE BIG INVESTMENT 211

Financial Pressure 211

Silencing Dissent 222

CHAPTER SEVEN

PROPOSALS FOR REFORM 231

A Few Modest Suggestions 231

Redefine "Of Age" 232

Separation of Functions 235

Break the Monopoly 240

Civil Service 244

CHAPTER EIGHT

GRASSROOTS CHANGE 247

Shaking Things Up 247

Unofficial Classes 248

Clubs and Organizations 251

Participating in Governance 257

Asking the Big Questions 261

ACKNOWLEDGEMENTS 267

REFERENCES 269

When I entered university in 2002, one of the first things I noticed was that a whole lot of students were disappointed. This may seem like an obvious observation, but I think it's one of the most significant facts about university today. Ask the average undergraduate if the experience is living up to his or her expectations. I'm sure some students out there are satisfied but I'm also willing to wager the great majority of them are not.

At first, I spent a lot of time ranting about various things that annoyed me and seemed absurd, or inadequate, or disappointing about university. Many students agreed with me and had frustrations and complaints of their own. But any time we tried to nail the problems down to concrete issues, we always found the discussion coming to an impasse simply because it was too vast. No matter what the initial subject happened to be — whether skyrocketing tuition, ballooning class size or the dumbing down of course content — if followed far enough the discussion would tend into abstract points and vague assertions about things that none of us really knew anything about. And so eventually, as with most issues that seem too vast or too complicated to grapple with, the discussions would always end with the defeated feeling that "that's just the way things are."

Let's say a student is upset by larger and larger class sizes that seem to have a negative effect on the quality of education. She might see reduced government funding as one cause. Then there's rising enrollment as more and more students continue to post-secondary education. Behind rising enrollment is the modern job market that seems to demand post-secondary degrees for even entry-level white-collar jobs. Along with rising enrollment comes the fact that universities are serving a "client base" unlike that which they served in the past. Behind government funding is a question of social spending priorities. And, well, by now our hypothetical student is probably sick of the question since there seem to be no clear answers. Her classes may be huge and over-enrolled but that's just the way it is. So she goes to class and makes the best of it, but not without a certain sense of frustration and a feeling of having been wronged in some indefinite way, of being cheated.

This book is intended to help undergraduate students in Canada, or those about to become undergraduate students, to cope with and get the most out of university. This book might also be of interest to those who care about students and prospective students, such as parents and educators, and also employers, and the government and ... well, let's face it, education is an important force in our society and it affects just about everyone. Quality education is still possible — and probably possible under the worst of circumstances — it's just a question of how hard you have to work to get it. My goal is to help students identify what they want out of university and then show them how they can best meet those objectives.

There are institutional problems with university today — problems that can't be entirely overcome simply through positive thinking or good advice. But the feelings of frustration that students experience, and the sense of being cheated, are problems by themselves. I'll talk quite a bit about the macro-level problems because I want to identify and explain them. It's hard to get the most out of university if you are constantly feeling let down by it. Even understanding things a little better can be a kind of solution. But this isn't a book about institutional reform. Change is needed and may come, in time, but it isn't going to happen overnight. Every September, a new class of students enters university and has to cope with the current reality, not the long-term vision. This book is for them.

When I set out to explain the problems at university, I ran into a serious roadblock. Even the students who are most unhappy don't agree with one another. Many feel that university education should be about exploring areas of interest, personal growth, and intellectual inquiry. Others feel that education should be about job skills and training. So already there's one major split among students over the question of practicality. Both groups of students are frequently unhappy, but for entirely different reasons. I can't claim, and be fair to everyone's feelings, that

> My goal is to help students identify what they want out of university and then show them how they can best meet those objectives.

university education is either too practical or not practical enough. And I don't want to make either claim anyway. What I want is to get at the root cause of why both groups are unhappy.

What is the source of this growing dissatisfaction with the university experience as a whole? To answer this question, I need to get at some root cause that embraces both the frustration felt by the student who wants to learn a profession and wishes for a more practical education, and the unhappiness felt by the student in the same class who wants a more generalist, abstract education. I must address the needs of the student who just wants time to figure things out without going broke in the process, and the next student at the same institution who knows exactly what kind of education he requires and is willing to pay whatever it takes to get it. For a time, this seemed to be an irresolvable contradiction, but in hindsight the answer is obvious, even self-evident. After all, how can we agree in one breath that we don't want the same things yet we all expect to get what we want from the same institution? That does seem a little strange, doesn't it?

University means so many different things to so many people that we sometimes imagine we are all talking about the same thing when we aren't. It isn't just a matter of the buildings or the instructors or the students all gathered together in the same place. What is the purpose of this thing called university? What's it doing?

Did we even agree in the first place on what the function of university is or should be?

When we say we aren't happy with our experiences at university, that's another way of saying we think the institution isn't performing its function very well on our behalf. But did we even agree in the first place on what that function is or should be?

So the first order of business, in Chapter One, is an overview of everything I believe university does. There are two ways to divide university into smaller components so we can talk about them separately. One way is to discuss university in terms of the *functions* it performs. The institution does a surprising number of things that quickly seem, when isolated, to be not very complementary to one another. The other way is to think of university in terms of the *people* who participate in it, and group them according to their goals and reasons for being there. These two systems interact freely because if university performs a variety of functions, and if people participate in university for a variety of reasons, most reasons can be aligned with one or more of the functions.

One more quick example. University provides accreditation, which is to say it provides degrees that certify what a particular graduate is presumed to have learned. It also provides education, which is to say it imparts knowledge. These two things are absolutely not the same. It must be obvious that a person can get a degree without learning much and can learn without getting a degree. So these are two broad things that university does. And many students who attend university immediately relate to one function or the other. Some students are there quite clearly to get their degrees (and some want the degree regardless of whether or not it represents any real education), while others are there simply to learn. Both these ways of thinking about university are useful and should help us come to grips with a topic that is otherwise so vast it seems impossible to even talk about.

It's entirely possible that one group of students who attend university looking for one thing will find themselves at cross purposes with another group of students who came looking for something else. Neither group is wrong. Both have arrived because they were promised their goals would be achieved through university education. But their different goals suggest entirely different sets of priorities and values. That's why there is this general sense of wrongness and dissatisfaction throughout the student population — without any consensus on exactly what is wrong.

Chapter Two continues with some practical information that should be of use to just about anyone attending university, and also a discussion of how the institution works. If you just want to consume education like any other product, you may wonder why you need to know how it's produced or delivered, especially since the large majority of students probably don't know how their education happens. You can pay for it and accept it, the same way you buy a drive-through burger, if you wish, with no thought for what's going on behind the window. Except with this particular purchase, you're investing tens of thousands of dollars and years of your life. When you are looking to buy, you might want to find out at least as much about your education as you would about, say, the new car market. When it comes to university, you will get more out of it if you know what's going on beneath the surface that every student sees.

Chapter Three is focused on helping you get the most out of your time at university. If you're tempted to skip right there, please don't. I'm not just wasting your time by going into functions and types of people at university. I'm trying to get you to think about what you want and where you fit in. Once you have a good idea about what you want out of university, I'll have suggestions about how to get more of it, but first you have to confront the tough questions. What do you want? Why did you show up to university in the first place? What are you trying to achieve? I can't give you a single formula for success, so first you have to think seriously about what success means to you.

Why did you show up to university in the first place? What are you trying to achieve?

Chapter Four deals with some specific problems and tries to explain things that often don't make sense to students. There are a lot of complaints out there about university, but it's amazing how often the same set of issues gets repeated — questions about grading, the role of private industry in the classroom, the relationship between students and faculty, and more. Probably I'll talk about some of the things that are bugging you. Everyone feels a little bit more comfortable when they know what's going on around them, and if you're going to spend years in university it's a good idea to get as comfortable as you can.

In Chapter Five, I've got the really big picture. Okay, you might not need to read this if you just want practical advice. But I promise there are ideas here you can apply to your immediate life as a student, and I hope I'll have hooked you into general interest in the subject anyway. Chapter Six is all about cost and effect. The cost of education today has so much impact it simply can't be overstated. I'll examine both what it means to students and what it means to society more generally. Chapter Seven is a nod toward large-scale reform. I know, I said this wasn't a book about fixing the whole system, and it isn't. I wish it were that easy. But after I identify all these problems, I feel as though I should offer at least some potential solutions.

Finally, in Chapter Eight, I've got some thoughts for shaking things up right where you are and right away. Why wait for major institutional reform? Change starts at home. You can get more out of your education and make it better for the people around you at the same time. Whatever you want more of, you can at least make some of it happen. And by the time you get this far I hope these suggestions will seem so natural you don't even need them anymore. Maybe you'll come up with initiatives I've never considered. But I'll at least offer some ideas to get you started.

When it comes to using this book, the bottom line is that the system isn't going to change overnight. We all have to deal with university, as it exists right now, whether it's ideal for our needs or not. I talk about the macro-level issues because understanding the problems of university can help everyone feel more in control of their experiences. But the focus will always be on the here and now, and how we can all get more of what we each want from education. So let's take an honest look at university, and get past the idea that it has a single coherent function or goal as an institution. Then we can see what's really going on.

CHAPTER ONE

THE FUNCTIONS OF EDUCATION

What Happens in a School

In order to understand university as it currently exists, it seems reasonable that we should take a moment to look at education as a whole, and figure out just what is being done and why. I don't intend to dwell on high school and elementary school, but when discussing education it's useful to remember that distinctions between various levels are artificial. High school ends after an arbitrary number of years and then university begins. A student goes to college or trade school to pursue one field of study but goes to university to learn another. Obviously these distinctions are the result of policy decisions, and can shift. Very recently in Ontario, a student would attend high school for five years but now it's four.[1] Everything shifted to accommodate that change. Our system of education, as a whole, serves various different roles at different times, so let's take a moment to look at all of what education does in broad terms. Then we can apply these ideas about education to what's going on at university.

The Holding Pen

In a real sense, especially for children, school provides a place to be that isn't at home, perhaps so both parents can work, or to give the homemaker a break. It's a place to be for anyone too young to enter the workforce. And as those kids grow into teenagers and young adults, the issue of when they are "old enough" to enter the workforce proves rather fluid. Realistically, they're old enough when the job market is ready to absorb them.

An interesting way to look at this "holding pen" concept is by referring to enrollment statistics in high school during periods of economic expansion, or recession and depression. As the job market dries up, as in the 1930s, teenagers stay in school longer. When job opportunities rebound, as in the late 1940s, students have less incentive to be in school. It isn't simply that students are dropping out because they are lured by the prospect of good wages; it's only a matter of how long they have to wait to get the same jobs they were heading toward anyway. A strong economy creates openings sooner rather than later. And in the meanwhile, kids stay in school because they've got to do something and education will help them compete down the road.

So is it only younger kids and teenagers who are in school because they have to be somewhere? I will argue that it absolutely is not, and that a lot of people stay in school through their late teens and into their early to mid twenties simply because there's no place for them in the workforce, or at least no place they are willing to accept. The only question is at what point that ends.

Teaching Good Citizenry

"Good citizenry" is a wide set of ideas I am lumping together — generally all of the things students learn in school that contribute to being better members of society. We associate citizenry all the time with early school, where kids learn to share, play nice, and work well with others. We also tend to believe there are some certain basic skills people require in order to function as full members of society, skills like literacy and essential math. These things are taught in school as a benefit to the students, certainly, but also for the good of society as a whole.

This function of early education also has a parallel that occurs in post-secondary schooling and this is often at the centre of the public funding debate. Is the higher education of someone good for society as a whole, entirely apart from direct economic results?[2]

Does a student in higher education learn social responsibility? Community involvement? In a democratic state founded on the principle of citizen involvement, these are not idle questions. Once again, what may seem to be a function of only early school touches on later schooling as well, right into university and other kinds of higher education.

Does a student in higher education learn social responsibility? Community involvement?

Certification of Basic Competence

One function of education is to train generally competent people, and to certify their abilities. This level of education has often been associated with a high school diploma. Beyond necessary life skills, this is the level of qualification that seems to suggest a student has gained certain basic abilities such as work ethic, analytic skills, an ability with written and spoken language, etc. Not to say that a person without a diploma lacks these skills, simply that the certificate formally recognizes them.

Certification of basic competence is possibly the biggest contribution that the education system makes to the private sector. Employers, obviously, have a strong vested interest in being able to identify potential employees who have this basic competence. And more besides, but I'll touch later on credentialism.

Now, let me reiterate what I mean by a certification of basic competence. This is the thing you put on your resumé as your base level of education. This is the degree that opens most employment doors (at least enough to apply) unless the job requires specialized knowledge or training. At one time this *was* a high-school diploma. No longer.

The current form of this certificate of competence is a university undergraduate degree or a college diploma. Some undergraduate degrees and college diplomas are also more than this, and include directed job skills aimed at specific careers, but a typical Bachelor of Arts or Science degree or a general arts diploma is just that. It gets your foot in the door. No more and no less.

Vocational Training

To discuss directed job training, I quite deliberately use a term that frequently conjures negative associations. What is vocational training? Training for a vocation, obviously — it's learning directed at landing and performing a specific kind of job. The words "vocational training" apply to the study of plumbing, journalism, computer programming, and dentistry, as well as any other kind of education you pursue in order to perform a specific job.

The major difference between various forms of vocational training is that some — such as dentistry — require a certificate of competence before you can begin these programs. Others — such as journalism — you might take as part of a certification of competence. Still others — such as plumbing — you might learn through apprenticeship, and outside of formal education entirely. But despite varying levels of status, income, and prestige associated with these jobs, the learning required to perform them is all *vocational training*. So what's the difference between a vocation and a profession? Income and status and not a lot else. Even income is an inconsistent standard, because a

So what's the difference between a vocation and a profession? Income and status and not a lot else.

skilled tradesperson will outearn a lot of professionals who are accorded more respect at your average cocktail party.

Obviously education is concerned with vocational training. This is now primarily at the post-secondary level, though secondary schools have long experimented with alternative academic programming aimed at those students not bound for further education in order to give them some employable skills. This is probably where the term "vocational training" gets its negative associations. At the high-school level, at least, it's often viewed as a sort of remedial program, and perhaps even implemented as one.[3] Despite these negative associations toward vocational training in high school, everyone knows and acknowledges that one of the reasons to go to university is to get a job, often a very specific job.

Pursuit of Knowledge

So what about learning something just for the sake of learning? This can happen at any level of education and common sense dictates the best students are inevitably the ones who are really interested in what they are learning, but this is almost always presented as a subordinate motivation to reach some other goal. Every teacher, from kindergarten upward, is concerned with finding ways to make learning fun. But these teachers are still pushing a set curriculum of what students are supposed to learn, and what's good for them. In university, probably for the first time, students encounter an environment that will validate almost any kind of learning or field

Probably for the first time, students encounter an environment that will validate almost any kind of learning.

of study, subject to standards of rigor and approach. Many professional academics work for their entire lives on research — supported through grants and teaching positions — that has no immediate practical application. But is that all there is to it?

Every student who comes to university and chooses to study something in whole or in part just because they are interested in it is involved in the pursuit of knowledge. It's rather alarming how natural it is to describe such a student as being "just interested" in a subject, as though that's a rather trivial reason to be in school. Why "just?" Many students study particular subjects out of interest but some are understandably sensitive about it. They tend to get questions like, "What are you going to do with *that*?" And everyone, of course, eventually has to confront the question of how to find work and put food on the table.

At the highest levels, the pursuit of knowledge and the need for a vocation eventually collide. Stay in school long enough and you end up as a professional (remember, that's code for "vocational") academic. And that's where professors come from. But it takes a lot of years beyond the undergraduate level to end up there and we're primarily interested in undergraduate university right now. Still, keep in mind that many professors are just students who never left university. It's a useful way to think of them.

University

"University" is such a loaded word. It describes many things at once, and many different people engaged in different sorts of work for unrelated reasons. In the sections to follow, I'll introduce some specific terms aimed at dividing university into particular functions and groupings of people that we can discuss separately, but for now let's look at the whole, and summarize, in rough terms, what is going on here.

First, university serves as a holding pen. When the average student finishes high school and realizes that the job prospects with a high-school diploma are basically flipping burgers or making lattes, university seems like the obvious alternative for anyone able to attend. I don't mean to deride the service sector, and I certainly don't mean to exclude those exceptional self-made success stories that are still happening today, I just want to clearly state that the high-school diploma is no longer the certification of basic competence that it once was. Other than as a gateway to higher education, it no longer opens many doors at all. When it comes to shopping around the job market, a high-school diploma is barely worth the paper it's printed on because almost any job that can be had with just a high-school diploma (typically not a good one) can be had just as easily without one. So students go to university, on some levels, for the same reason they attended kindergarten. They don't yet have a place to be (in this case, in the workforce) and need to be somewhere.

Second, university is that certification of basic competence that high school once was. Quite a lot of students go to university, graduate from some Bachelor of Arts or Science program, and then go on to careers entirely unrelated to what they studied, except that the degree opened the door for them. This is not at all unprecedented. It wasn't so very long ago that Latin was a required course in Ontario high schools.[4] So when a high-school diploma was the certificate of basic competence, did that mean employers were looking for employees who could read Latin? Of course not. And when a student with a B.A. in English goes on to work in the business field, it isn't because a thorough knowledge of Shakespeare is much help either. It's what the degree represents more than the substance of the course content, and no matter what area that degree is in, it can and should pay off eventually.[5]

Third, university is a continuation of the lessons of good citizenry begun in early schooling. This aspect is sometimes difficult to see from outside university life, but can be very obvious from within it. There is a reason political movements — everything from gender equity, environmental causes, and voting reform — are based around university campuses. There is a reason student leaders are often at the forefront of social change. The university environment provides, for those who look for it, an opportunity to practice in immediate and meaningful terms the sort of citizen involvement that forms the basis of a healthy democracy. Not every student will take advantage of this, and some might not even see it around them as they pass from class to class, but the atmosphere is there all the same — even in the most anemic university environments.

Fourth, university provides vocational training or preparation for it. This is the part of university that people most often see. This is the part of university that the private sector wants to get their hooks into. Take any industry that isn't subject to professional

> University provides an opportunity to practice the sort of citizen involvement that forms the basis of a healthy democracy.

regulation as an example. Journalism is a textbook case. Why is a university degree, or college diploma, required to practice journalism? Simply because no media publisher is eager to hire a journalist without some kind of degree, unless he or she is already known as a writer. This wasn't always the case.[6] My major point is that it's a self-regulating standard. The journalism industry, by virtue of demanding that any job applicant attend college or university in order to become a journalist, has effectively handed a monopoly over the gateway to the industry to colleges and universities. And that's interesting.

Finally, university serves as a place where people — whether students or faculty — pursue knowledge for its own sake. Depending on whose opinion you ask, this can be the majority of what universities do even today, or it can be a minor function left over from less productive days before universities really got down to the business of producing employable units. I believe that, while few students in university today are occupied in the pursuit of knowledge exclusive to other goals, this activity still forms a background priority in the purposes of many other students. The majority of those whose goals are purely job-oriented have not turned their backs entirely on the established wisdom of finding a job that interests them, and any student that is interested in his or her subject is engaged, to some extent, in learning for its own sake. So this aspect of university is certainly not gone, it's just tangled up with a lot of other priorities, much like the institution itself.

Why Go to University?

Nothing aggravates me more than talking about university with people who don't even know why they are there. It isn't the students who annoy me, it's the entire idea that anyone could go through high school, talk with guidance counsellors, teachers, friends, and family, could apply for government loans and sign into debt, and still not have an answer as to why it happened. It isn't the students who have failed, it's the entire system. It seems incredible to think that anyone could invest years of time, and tens of thousands of dollars, with no clear purpose to justify all that effort and expense, but it happens all the time.

Some students will claim they've gone to university to "be successful." That isn't an answer. Success means lots of different things to different kinds of people and in many cases it doesn't require university at all. If you want to study something because you are really interested in it, then say that. If you are looking for a specific kind of job, then say that instead. But acting as though university is the one and only ticket to success in life is both simplistic and flawed. It's another way of saying you went to university because you were scared not to, and you're not quite sure why you are there, but you know the alternatives aren't attractive. That's an answer too, though a problematic and potentially dangerous one.

It's never too late or too early to ask the important questions, so let's start with this one. Why go to university? I've suggested broad categories of the various things university is and does, so presumably if you've gone to university you are there to get one or more of those things. Let's look at them again.

Pure Learning

Some people are just interested in certain things and want to learn about them, and university seems a likely place to do that. Opinions about this particular function of university are mixed. Parents, students, and even administrators and faculty are divided on the subject. Some think this is the only good reason to run a university, and that any other purpose is a dilution of this goal. Others think this is an outdated idea and one that doesn't have much place in modern education. Some parents I've met would love nothing more than to discover their son or daughter is passionate about the study of English, philosophy, or something similar. Others would almost faint over the idea, followed immediately by a sort of an accusatory question, "What kind of job are you going to get with that?!" I suspect you already have some ideas of your own on this subject. When someone tells you they are studying something because they're interested in it, does that strike you as a good reason, or do you tend to think it's frivolous?

There probably aren't many undergraduate students in university today who are only interested in learning for its own sake. It would be nice to think there were more, but let's face it, the percentage of people who do anything in this world only because they love it is pretty small. Still, these aren't intended to be exclusive categories of motivation, and I would suggest there are more people motivated by love of learning than is frequently assumed. If you've ever studied something or taken a course even partly because it looked interesting, then you were motivated by a desire to learn. You don't need to be idealistic to make this choice because common sense backs it up. You'll always be better at things you find interesting, so you should take advantage of that whenever possible.

What are you interested in, curious about, or motivated to learn? If you don't have any immediate answers that's okay, but consider that you are at a bit of a disadvantage at any institution of higher learning if you have no particular interest in learning. There are other ways to get motivated, but interest is a big one. And if an opportunity arises to take something that interests you and somehow turn it into a career, don't write off that option lightly — it's an opportunity too few people have.

> To take something that interests you and somehow turn it into a career is an opportunity too few people have.

Career Training

When universities offer undergraduate programs called "management," or "pharmacology," or "early teacher training," it's hard to escape the awareness that universities have bought into the business of career preparation in a big way. As always, there are extreme opinions on either side. Some alarmists see this as the end of "real" education entirely, while others seem to think education is all about meeting the needs of industry and the job market. The truth is doubtless somewhere in between, as it usually is. There's a need for certain kinds of vocational training, and for better or for worse, that's going on at university these days. But is that why you are there?

Some people will say that university is about getting a good job, and I'm sure you are aware of the way your prospects will be improved by your degree. But do you actually know which job you want, or do you just know which income bracket? If you've got a job at least mostly in mind, if you know what kind of skills you want and what kind of field you see yourself in, then you are probably looking for a career out of university. If you are just trying to avoid flipping burgers and taking the bus to work, well, that's a reason too, but you don't have a career in mind. You're just thinking about a lifestyle.

If you know what you want to do with your life, that's great. University takes a lot of time, and a lot of effort, and it's awfully hard to get through it with much success if you don't know why. I hope your career goals have at least something to do with your skills and interests, because it's easy to get seduced by lifestyle, and even when you are aiming for a specific profession your ideas of it may be totally divorced from the reality of the work. Medicine and law are major culprits here. Maybe you've also been influenced by your parents' ideas of what they'd like to tell their friends about you. We all know, quite honestly, those are bad reasons to get into a field, but if you've got a career in mind, that's a concrete goal, and a reason to be in university. And that's more than many students have. If you care about it enough to stay motivated, you're ahead of the game.

Life Experience

So even if you aren't in love with a specific area of study or with pursuit of a particular career, that doesn't mean you can't gain from university, right? People say it's also the place you can go when you *don't* know what you want because it will help you straighten everything out. It's a learning experience, an opportunity to grow, and so on. After a couple of years, it will all make sense. Just wait and see.

Okay, all of this is true to some extent. Just because you don't know what you want to do with your life, or what you are really interested in learning, doesn't mean you *aren't* interested in learning, or that you plan on doing nothing with your life. Parents, counsellors, and sitcoms have used this reasoning for decades to point bright but otherwise under-motivated students toward university in the hope they'll figure it out on the way to their degrees. We tend to allow there's some logic to this. I'm sure it works, at least some of the time.

If you are at university because it seemed like the best place to figure out your life, that's a reason like any other, but it comes with some serious dangers. When you are in classes you don't especially care about, and aren't sure why you're taking, you aren't likely to do all that well. How well do you need to do, anyway? That's hard to say if you don't know what you want out of life.

> If you are at university because it seemed like the best place to figure out your life, that's a reason like any other, but it comes with some serious dangers.

If you just want to finish with a degree, you don't need to do very well to manage that. If you want to get into a graduate program later, that's a whole other standard of "doing well." So you've got a reason to be in university, at least for now, but it might not be enough by the time you are done.

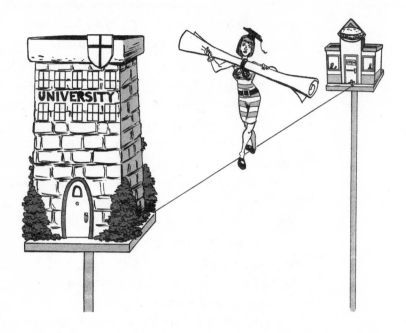

Not Flipping Burgers

For all those people who can't say what they want in terms of a career, but know for damn sure what they don't want, the undergraduate degree (or in some cases the college diploma) is just a way to get away from that. It's the basic certification, the foot in the door, the ticket to at least white-collar respectability, assuming you don't screw it up. And for any teenager emerging from high school with no direction in life, continuing schooling seems like a far better option, if it's available, than working at the shop down the street. This is certainly a reason to be at university even if it's grounded mostly in fear. Let's be honest here. If I ask you why you are in university, and you think more about the things you want to avoid in life than the things you want, or else focus immediately on the things you'd like to buy rather than on how you plan on earning your living, you've got some hard questions to think about.

For better or for worse, it's true that university has become, for many people, the place to gain basic certification. If that's why you decided to attend university, it's an answer at least, and a place to start, but it isn't enough to last. Fear and knowledge of what you don't want can only carry you so far. Will it carry you through the years required to graduate? Will it be enough for you to compete with the students around you who aren't necessarily any smarter or better than you but are more motivated? It's something to consider.

Fear and knowledge of what you don't want can only carry you so far.

No Clue

There are a shocking number of students in university who would be stunned by the idea that one needs a reason to be there. For them, there are things in life you just don't question. At some stage, you finish grade eight, and the next year a bus comes and takes you to high school. You don't ask why, you just go. And in many cases, the transition to university is managed just as smoothly by parents, friends, and surrounding people who always assumed it would happen. You don't ask why, you just fill out your applications, maybe sign the loan documents, and go. I'm really not kidding.

Now, the unfortunate part about this is probably none of these people would think to read a book about what's wrong with university or how they can get more out of it. If you know people like this, hit them over the head with a copy of this book, and maybe they'll think about it. Or better yet, just ask them the same questions I'm asking you right now. "Why did you come to university? What are you looking to get out of this?" That might be the most important thing anyone says to them all year.

Just like anything else in life, it's possible to surf though university with a minimum amount of effort and attention. Some choose to focus instead on pastimes and hobbies, relationships and family, because it's so much more interesting and keeps the rest bearable. As the quality of surrounding students improves (as it does in later years), it gets harder to scrape by with this minimal effort, but some people seem to manage. Others flunk out. But life doesn't end with graduation, and a degree in hand — even for those who achieve it on autopilot — won't tell you what to do next. So the sooner you work out where you want to go, the sooner you can start steering in that direction, rather than hope you end up there by accident.

Life doesn't end with graduation, and a degree in hand won't tell you what to do next.

Which Is Right?

No function of university is necessarily better or worse than any of the others. They all respond to various needs in society. And no student is in university for the "right" reason to the exclusion of all others, though some might be there for poor reasons. Let's take it for granted that all the things universities are doing today occur because there is some need for them. People want to learn, find jobs, take some time to straighten out their lives, prove their competence; they all deserve a place to do that. But it obviously doesn't need to be the *same* place. Yet that's what we've got, and we call it a modern university.

If university feels screwed up because it's trying to do too many things at once for too many kinds of people with different reasons for being there, that's a problem. In my opinion, it's *the* problem. Just remember your fellow students aren't the root cause of any frustration you may feel. Blaming the people

around you, just because they've got attitudes, goals, and intentions that don't fit well with yours, is a dead-end path. We've all been ill-served by a system that throws us together in the same blender with the vague expectation things will just sort themselves out. But at least it's something we can cope with. It just takes some extra effort to think about what we each want and figure out how to get it, instead of getting a whole lot of what the next student wants, which is probably something entirely different.

1 The removal of one year from the high-school curriculum in Ontario came as part of a comprehensive change in 1999. This change is laid out in detail in a government document called *Ontario Secondary Schools, Grades 9–12: Program and Diploma Requirements.* Universities throughout Ontario continue to adjust to the resulting changes in the student demographic entering first year.

2 Economists wrangle endlessly over how to calculate the social returns on education. The cost of providing it is easy to determine. Public revenue in the form of economic production can be tallied. But attempts to measure social gains in terms of greater health, happiness, and public awareness defy conventional analysis. As do any number of additional factors, such as the advantages gained by children of more educated parents who may learn from them at home. Nevertheless, economists do attempt to either calculate these gains in dollars and cents, or else justify their omission, as part of the continuing debate surrounding appropriate levels of public investment. See *The Economic Value of Higher Education* (Leslie and Brinkman) for a good overview of this discussion.

3 Some theorists critique vocational education in secondary schools from the view that much of it is aimed at producing a second-class tier of employee, deferential and resigned to limited opportunities in life. From this view, career training at the post-secondary level is very different, and geared toward upward mobility rather than stagnation. For a more complete discussion of vocational training in Canada, see Coulter and Goodson's *Rethinking Vocationalism: whose work/life is it?*

4 Introductory Latin, a grade-nine course, was removed from the Ontario high-school curriculum in 1949 under the Porter Plan.

5 In "A Matter of Discipline: Early Career Outcomes of Recent Canadian University Graduates," Ross Finnie compares rates of employment and earnings by academic discipline over an extended period. He finds that students from a background in fine arts and humanities often experience short-term difficulties finding stable employment and start with lower salaries. But five years after graduation, their rates of unemployment are no worse than other fields, and their salaries, while still slightly on the low side, have closed the gap considerably.

6 Journalism is a field where considerable debate has occurred (and continues) within the profession regarding the best and most appropriate preparation for a career journalist. College programs appeal to students and employers who favour emphasis on concrete skills while university programs appeal to a competing school of thought that favours a broad foundation in the liberal arts. For a very long time, many held the only effective preparation was on-the-job training. Tom Dickson provides an excellent history of this dialogue in *Mass Media Education in Transition.*

CHAPTER TWO

THE MODERN UNIVERSITY

How Does It Happen?

I'll get tired of pointing this out eventually, but we are talking about years of your life, and tens of thousands of dollars of your money. If you're receiving loans, it may not feel like real money, but trust me, it will when you have to start paying it back. If you're fortunate enough to have your education paid for by relatives who care about you, that's even better, but it's still a huge chunk of real money spent on you. And if you're working to pay for your education while you receive it ... well, then I'm not saying anything you don't already know, right? When you're earning eight or ten dollars an hour (maybe more, if you're lucky), it isn't hard to see how many hours of your life that tuition represents. In return for this very large investment, I imagine you have a natural interest in what you receive. You are paying for this education, so let's talk about how it gets delivered and what form it takes.

Professors

The people most responsible for delivering your education are the ones standing at the front of the classroom. So it's in your best interest to know something about your professors — as a group, if not as individuals. One of the first things even the most clueless student learns is that you don't call a professor "Mr.," "Mrs.," or "Ms." If you haven't started university yet, that's a good lesson to learn in advance. Anyone who has gone to the considerable trouble to earn a Ph.D. has earned the right to be called "Dr." instead. "Professor" works perfectly well also, and is usually the preferred term. Once in a while, you might get an instructor who has not yet completed a Ph.D. and is also not a professor in any formal sense, and you'll end up using a different form of address. But it's safest to start with "professor" and wait for correction.

Professors may be employed in a variety of ways, but tenure is the ultimate goal of most career academics. Those without it are fairly low on the university food chain. Tenured professors perform multiple functions as the basis of their employment. They teach classes, obviously. They also administrate, within their areas, and are responsible for various management-type functions. And they conduct research, which many professors consider the most important thing they do. This bears repeating because the people who are teaching you may not consider teaching their most important responsibility. The professional standing and success of a career academic depends more on their research

> The professional standing and success of a career academic depends more on their research than on their ability to teach.

than on their ability to teach. It's a hell of a system, isn't it?

Some think of tenure as simply some of the best job security around. A professor with tenure is pretty much guaranteed (barring some extreme event) employment until he or she retires. But this deal — and it is a pretty sweet deal — isn't simply the result of great contract negotiation. Professors receive tenure so they can conduct their research as they see fit, even if it isn't popular or commercially useful. Research can also become controversial, and tenure exists to protect the freedom of inquiry at the highest level. It's about learning for its own sake. And if you too are interested in learning for its own sake, you'll probably find that pretty cool. If not, you might wonder how that helps you get a job or do anything else with your life. In a lot of cases it doesn't, but hey, I did tell you university is a conflicted institution.

Instructor or Researcher?

One of the questions I like to ask students, if only to get a sense of their priorities, is "If you could learn from either a fun and entertaining instructor who is good at presenting the course material, or else from an international authority who is breaking new ground with research but is pretty boring in the classroom, which would you prefer?" There isn't a right or a wrong answer to this question, but it goes to the heart of the whole teaching versus research problem. A brilliant instructor is not necessarily a brilliant researcher, or vice versa. There are those who claim that university is a place where students are *taught*, and they need engaging instructors to help them learn, regardless of whether or not those instructors are on the cutting edge of innovation. Then there are those who claim that university is a place where students *learn*, and they should have the absolute best resources for learning. From this perspective, the faculty is just another resource, and a dry professor is not different from a dry textbook. The knowledge is there and it is the onus of the student to extract it. You don't assign a simpler textbook just because it's easier and more fun to read; you assign the best one available and leave it up to the students to get as much out of it as they can.

This whole teaching versus research issue is shot right through university. Even the administration of any particular institution probably doesn't have a concrete position. Which is the central mission? According to some, undergraduate students are almost a necessary evil, and their tuition is merely a way to subsidize and enable the research function of university. To others, teaching is the main purpose, and research is a way to gain reputation and standing for one's institution, and to entice the interest of the best students. From a middle perspective, it's a chicken-and-egg cycle, and one serves the other no matter where you start.

Research isn't something professors do because they necessarily like it — though most do, I would assume — or because it's a way to make money on the side, but rather because it's a central aspect of their jobs. In most cases, tenured professors are expected to conduct meaningful research and produce recognized results in their fields. As I said, there's no obligation to be popular or commercial. In fact entire fields exist that get very little public recognition and have limited application, but professors are still expected to be productive according to the standards of their respective disciplines. The odd thing about how professors work at the highest levels is there's no single authority that can approve or disapprove of anyone's results. That's why the concept of "peer review" is very important. The various experts working in a particular area regulate and judge each other, often with controls in place to ensure as much objectivity as possible. The professional academic who can impress his or her peers the most advances, and though it may be painful for students to hear this, the status of that accomplishment means more to most career professors than popularity in the classroom, or what a room full of undergraduates thinks about their lesson plans.

"Teachers"

Despite the status and the deeply ingrained traditions of tenure, the face of university instruction is changing. Pressures from rising enrollment and the changing student demographic are pushing more and more universities toward hiring "teaching-stream" faculty (often called lecturers or tutors) for the sole purpose of teaching classes, with no expectation of research production. Depending on your perspective, this represents either a sad dilution of the quality of higher education, or else is exactly what the system needs to serve students better.[1]

In many vocational fields, industry professionals — working experts in their areas — are recruited as lecturers on a part-time or full-time basis. In management or commerce, this might mean recruiting a marketing professional to teach classes in that area. In visual or performing arts, this might mean a working artist. In many cases, the opportunity to work with instructors who come from practical backgrounds is a huge draw for any student interested in pursuing a specific career. The opposite side of this rosy picture, where lecturers or teaching-stream instructors bring real-world experience into the classroom, is when these positions are simply used to reduce overhead — to hire someone with fewer credentials to teach twice as many courses for less money than it would take to pay a research-stream professor. Because this does occur, teaching-stream faculty frequently gain an undeserved reputation for being somehow lesser than research-stream faculty.

The other thing you'll sometimes get at the front of the classroom are temporary instructors who aren't part of the permanent faculty at all. Sad to say, but like temporary employees anywhere, these are used because they are easy to add and remove as a flexible workforce, and because they are cheap. Sometimes they're graduate students still completing their Ph.D.'s, and sometimes they're not different from other professional academics, except that they haven't landed long-term jobs yet, and may never. Just like anyone else, sometimes they are wonderful instructors, and sometimes they aren't. It's probable the overall quality of instruction is lower, since the hiring practices are much more rushed. But depending on your priorities, there's nothing wrong with academic "temps," as long as they are good instructors.

How It Runs

Just in terms of how it's run and administered, university is a pretty freaky place. Probably nothing else in the world runs like a modern university. Take any billion-dollar enterprise, put it in the hands of people who aren't trained to be administrators, throw in a lot of generally left-wing ideals (we are talking about academics after all), factor in government regulations, accommodate some demands from industry, and you've got a modern university. So if it seems a bit weird at times, that probably shouldn't be surprising.

As I mentioned earlier, part of the job description for tenured faculty is that they help administrate their departments and programs. Most of this is done at a relatively low level, where professors sit on committees, or participate in program and course design. But then someone needs to chair the department, and that's always a professor. And someone needs to be dean, and that's a professor too. The majority of the senior administration is drawn from faculty. Universities employ a lot of professional managers and business people to run things too, but at the top of almost every chain there's a professional academic. Most of them don't find much time to be real academics anymore (meaning their research gets pushed aside), and they end up running their universities sort of the same way professional athletes are converted into coaches and managers. So I guess you could say they learn how to manage while on the job. Still, the result is that somehow a background in physics, or anthropology, or linguistics, turns into the

At the top of almost every chain there's a professional academic.

foundation used to run a billion-dollar enterprise.

Professional academics don't want to surrender their academic freedom, and they don't trust anyone else to regulate them. In idealistic fashion, they tend to assume they know what's best for university. This does tend to leave professors and administrators vulnerable to the claim they've lost touch with reality, but at least this idealism extends to the wider university community. There's this wonderful idea that discussion and decision-making should include all "stakeholders" — everyone who stands to gain or lose. Typically this means lots of people, and so you end up with committees where all the appropriate groups are represented — some combination of faculty, staff, librarians, administration, alumni, and students.

There are committees, committees, and more committees. There are subcommittees, task forces, special commissions, working groups, boards, and councils. Almost anything that happens in a university can be traced back to some kind of body that made the decision or debated the issue — often at considerable length. Even when decisions are the responsibility of individual administrators, they probably report back to some group that could, theoretically, overrule them. And students sit on a remarkable number of these bodies. Probably a lot of the representation you receive as a student gets filtered through your students' union or administrative council, so if you are interested in all that, you should start there. But even if you don't want to get involved in the administration of your university, it's worth knowing how it works. If something stupid happens, there is always somewhere you can appeal. If someone claims nothing can be done, but you think you've got common sense and justice on your side, you can eventually find someone who will agree with you.

Remember, when dealing with any professor in a position of administrative authority, that they are trained to be open to opposing viewpoints, as long as they are backed by sound reasoning. Not only that, but you are dealing with someone doing a job for which they have no formal qualifications. If you disagree with your chemistry professor on a point of science, you'll probably never win. The fact is she's simply far better versed in the area than you are. But let's assume that same professor is chair of the chemistry department, and you have a disagreement with her over a university regulation of some sort, there is every possibility that you might be right, and she'll probably see things your way if you can field a solid argument. If you don't know how to go about doing that, there's probably a student representative somewhere, or a university advisor, who can take up the case for you. As I said, universities are strange sometimes. You might need to recruit some help, but you *can* come out on top if you need to argue over something. Just be sure you've got all your bases covered, because trained or not these people are pretty smart.

And You Are Learning From ... ?

You can be a full-time university student and have all of ten or fifteen hours of classes each week, depending on your program, local standards, and time-table. Some students act as though that means more time left for drinking and partying, but realistically we all know what the time is for. If learning is a full-time commitment, and you've only got ten or fifteen hours of class, what are you doing the other thirty-plus hours per week? Of course the short answer is "studying," but let's talk a moment about what that means.

You are learning from textbooks, you are learning from professors and instructors both in and out of the classroom, and you are learning from the students around you. Sometimes you'll be assigned to work with other students. You might also be aware of informal study groups, which some students find very helpful. And then there are times when learning from fellow students is a lot less systematic and involves begging a roommate at 5 a.m. to proofread an essay that's due at 9 a.m. Often students get the idea this sort of peer learning is accidental, as though they get "stuck" learning from the people around them because the professor is too busy, or the book is too boring, or they just don't have anyone else to turn to. It isn't accidental. The system is designed to work this way.

At university, you are supposed to be learning from your lectures and tutorials, and obviously you should pay close attention to the qualified people at the front of the class. But you are also expected to pull information out of the readings on your own, do additional research where necessary, and you are even expected to be able to sit down with your fellow students and peers, and help each other to figure out what maybe none of you fully understands alone. Depending on your perspective, this is either a great incentive toward maturity, striking out on your own, and really delving into education, or it's just a really cheap service-delivery model. Probably it's both.

This whole idea of leaving students on their own at university to learn or not learn, to pass or fail based on their own inclination to study and self-motivate, seems brutal to some people. Students feel abandoned, as though no one cares about their success anymore. Well, the good news is: that isn't really true. Lots of people care, and if you take the time to seek help with your studies, you'll find help. It's true the system is brutal, but not intentionally so. There is an assumption that you want to learn, and are able to do things on your own. A lot of this book is aimed at helping you find or isolate your goals in university so you can stay motivated. On a personal level, it's counter-productive to blame "the system" — even if there's a kernel of truth in the idea your university might not be doing enough for you. If you aren't motivated to learn, then no one can do enough for you. So put aside that gripe at least long enough to figure out what you want, and why you want it. Then, once you are making a sincere effort to extract that experience from your education, you can get angry again if you aren't getting enough of it.

How Does It Get Measured?

Constant evaluation has become a reality of modern education. You get graded for just about everything, and the grade, for many students, is the final goal. Some find this continual evaluation to be a real turnoff, while others are reassured by it — a consequence of differing motives. I'll talk about what this constant evaluation means to your goals later; for now let's just look at how grading works. I can't promise your grades will improve simply because you understand more about where they come from, but it can't possibly hurt.

Competition and the Curve

One of the ugly realities about education is that you are in competition with the students around you for your grades. If you are looking for a "good" grade, you've got to realize that everyone else is too, and not everyone can get one. Your institution has at least some standard, whether formal or informal, enforcing an expected distribution of grades. This could be as simple as a rough class average the professor must keep an eye on, or as complex as a whole list of parameters involving so many A's, so many B's, etc.[2] If you want to know exactly what kind of policy your school is using, do some digging. The standards are probably not public, but I guarantee they are there somewhere. Ask a professor or two. Many students dislike the idea that, in order for them to "win," someone else has to "lose," and even administrators are often inclined to gloss over this truism, but it's the entire concept of grading that creates competition. While we might be tempted to reject the idea, we all know on some level that constant evaluation implies competition against the people around us.

The idea of a "good" grade is completely relative. What is an A paper, anyway? Who sets the standard? Where does the idea of a "good" essay come from? Obviously there's only one answer. Good is better than average. And average is what most students will produce in a typical class. So whether we use numbers or letters, and regardless of *which* numbers and letters, the idea of "good" will always mean "better than the average student," just as "poor" will mean "worse than the average student." We can shift the scale and it won't make any difference. We can give a whole class of hundreds of students grades of 80% or above, but if we do that we are just using 80% to represent the worst student in the class; nothing changes. People will still know which grade represents the worst student in the class, and will attach the appropriate meaning.

It's tempting to think a large class of students can all get good grades, but that only introduces a new problem by expanding the sample group. A class of hundreds of students might all receive unusually high grades, but now the good performance of that class is only "good" relative to the standards of the whole school. So if the average across your university is 65%, and a class of hundreds comes out with an average of 85%, then sure, they all got good grades. But that's exactly why a curve is enforced. Unless there's something fabulously unusual about that class, it's simply not fair to the rest of the school to represent their performance on a different scale. The idea of a good grade is still regulated by the institutional average.

Maybe an entire school could skew their grades and graduate everyone with near perfect grade point averages, but that only devalues the reputation of the school itself, which is another kind of control. Regardless, the idea of a high grade is still relative to what other institutions are doing, and if they all did the same thing, it wouldn't mean anything anymore. This problem does creep up on institutions sometimes, and that's why administrators guard against the dangers of grade inflation. They also consider their average relative to other institutions. If it helps at all, every school will certainly have some process or other to accommodate an exceptional situation. If, for example, an entire class of students *is* unusually good (or unusually bad) there will be some way to turn in an unusual set of grades. But this still acknowledges the idea of what's "normal."

If all of this strikes you as somehow unfair, I'm not surprised. Most students I've met either tend to relate to this information naturally, and accept it right away, or else they never get comfortable with the idea, and tend to feel there's something intentionally cruel and arbitrary happening. Either way, since you are going to have to live with the system, you might as well understand it. It might save you some grief.

"Easy" Courses

Once you digest the idea of a grading curve it will probably torpedo the notion of easy courses. Students express their faith in the existence of easy courses lots of ways. They ask for bird courses, GPA boosters, whatever. Quite often students go looking for these courses to recover from whatever kind of academic holes they've gone and dug for themselves. And the sad thing is, more often than not, anyone aiming for an easy course is going to screw up his situation worse than it was screwed up in the first place. If you don't believe anything else, please believe this.

Remember that a good grade has nothing to do with the material covered in the course — at least not in terms of its difficulty. In order to get a good grade, you need to do better than the students around you. If the material for a particular course is easy, then it's easy for everyone. Sure a course can look simple on paper, but everyone in that class is taking exactly the same course, and the class average is going to look much the same as the average for any other class. So how exactly is that going to help you? If you have a natural interest in the subject, or an aptitude for the area, then that counts for something. It's not news that students who are interested or talented in a particular area tend to do well. What we are talking about here is the illusion that somehow everyone in a particular course can get an easy ride. That's simply not true. Worse, the idea that this is possible motivates students to take courses entirely outside of their fields based on some rumour that they're easier. And that's when things go really wrong.

Accept it as a given that in any subject area there will be interested and talented students. You can take a music class as an elective, or a philosophy class, or whatever, and you may consider the material covered in the class to be a joke, but I promise many of the other students in that class won't consider it a joke. They are motivated, and interested, and what have you got going for you? You just showed up for an easy class. And damn, are you ever going to be annoyed when you find that not only is the class not

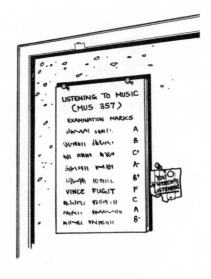

easy, but now you are stuck working extra hard to learn something you don't care about. It's no wonder students end up doing poorly, or even failing, in the classes that attract a reputation for being easy. Examples that haunt the students of my old campus include "Listening to Music" and "Children's Literature."[3] I'm positive students take these classes just because the titles make them sound easy. And they do sound easy, don't they? Don't be fooled.

From beginning to end, it's just a bad idea to take a course because you think it will be easy. If you believe in the grading curve (and I promise, it's real), the only excuse you have to take a course and think it will be easy is if you have no respect for the students in that program. Now, apart from the fact that this is simply rude, let's go ahead and assume it isn't a very strong program, that the entrance average is low, and you hope you can outperform most other students in the class. You are still challenging people at their own game, outside of your subject area, and playing away from your natural strengths. So it's still a bad idea. Just don't do it. Take courses outside your area(s) if you have interest on your side, sure, but never take something only because you hope it will be easy.

Subjective versus Objective Grading

Another thing about grading that tends to really throw students is the difference between subjective grading standards and objective ones. Most programs, and most student preferences, fall firmly into one camp or the other. Take your average math or science course and an answer is either right or wrong. Typically speaking, math and science students really like it that way. The idea of an essay just terrifies them, and not necessarily because they are bad writers, but because there's no sure way to know what's "right." Similarly, if you take your average course in English, or philosophy, or similar subjects, precise standards of right and wrong have gone straight out the window. Of course there are still very real standards to distinguish between good and poor work, but you can't study from a textbook and know exactly what to say. Multiple-choice exams in English and philosophy are no one's idea of a good time, nor an effective method of evaluation. So which testing method is better? More important, which is fairer? Well, neither obviously, they're just different ways of grading, but the interesting thing is how similar they really are if you push far enough.

Math and science students, with their objective grading standards, almost never have to be told about the grading curve. They see it in action. You take a test, and if everyone does too well, you divide the total by 1.05 or whatever to drive the average down. If everyone does badly, you increase the average in a similar way. After a while, a good instructor will learn how to format a test to produce the average that's required, but don't lose sight of the fact it's still happening. Arts students, who don't see that kind of grading, often don't realize there's a curve at all, though sometimes they'll ask questions like "Where did I lose marks on my paper?" This sort of question just reveals a basic misunderstanding of what's happening. You don't end up with 82% on an essay because you lost 18% in specific places. You

You don't end up with 82% on an essay because you lost 18% in specific places.

end up with 82% because you were better than many students, but not as good as some. You should get some comments back about where and how you can improve your writing, and things you might have done to get a better grade, but there's no point trying to add those comments up to equal the 18% you "lost."

Students will almost always express a preference for either subjective grading systems or objective ones. Those who argue in favour of subjective methods usually emphasize the fact that these methods are individualized, and focus on understanding rather than memorization. And grading can be a lot more forgiving with part marks and credit for reasonable effort. Those who argue in favour of objective methods usually emphasize certainty, and the ability to know exactly what is required. But remember the ultimate standard of what it takes to get a good grade is simply to be better than the students around you. If you don't like the form of grading in use, but you are genuinely interested in the subject and you think you can do well at it, don't let the methods of evaluation deter you. Your performance can still shine through either way.

Institutional Reputation

When you work through the implications of the whole grading-curve issue, and realize that some institutions naturally attract better students (who in turn become your competition), it's hard to escape the next obvious conclusion. If you wanted to get higher grades, you should have gone to a weaker school!

Students who enroll in a particular school or program because it has a good reputation sometimes feel cheated once they get a handle on the whole grading-curve issue, especially if they aren't doing very well on that curve. It's hard to measure the value of institutional reputation. Most people agree it's there, but how does it pay off, and just how much is it worth? And that question, I'm afraid, is one that even the experts will never agree on, so I'm not able to give you an answer. Your institution's reputation is sustained, in part, because it doesn't hand out A's like candy, and that's where students end up feeling a lot of frustration. They feel like their school is actually conspiring against them just to maintain the idea that it's a top school.

There's a balance. Where that balance occurs is impossible to illustrate, but the only way to really be fair to students is to maintain a consistent standard. Your school's reputation, whatever it may be, was built on certain expectations of the students that came before you. If those standards suddenly loosened, you could benefit at the expense of everyone who came before, and profit from the reputation without meeting the same expectations. If those standards suddenly tightened, you could suffer in a similar way. So realistically, a consistent standard with perhaps very long-term trends is the only way an institution can possibly be "fair." Unlike high schools, which attract local students and therefore have a certain average that's expected across the system, post-secondary institutions draw from self-selected groups of applicants. So a B average from a university program that's attracting top students means more than a B average from a university program that's further down the hierarchy of reputation. How will that play out for you in terms of your personal, educational, and career goals? Exactly how does this get accounted for by the graduate and professional schools you may apply to in the future? Again, I can't measure it out for you because every school, every employer, every program and its entrance standards, will consider your academic record differently. If it helps to know that institutional reputation factors into those decisions in many places to compensate for differing standards of competition, well, it does, and I can promise it's there, and that's about it.

What Do You Get?

There are basically two things you get out of your investment in university education. You get the learning itself and you get the official seal of the university that vouches for what you've learned. It's easy to confuse the two, but certainly it's possible to get one without the other, so they obviously aren't the same thing. We can all think of examples of people who have graduated with no significant learning to show for it (some even boast about it), and of course it's possible to learn something and not receive a stamp to prove what you know. Nevertheless, the deal at university is you get both, or at least you are supposed to.

University doesn't have a monopoly on learning and you could probably learn a lot of things both cheaper and maybe even better on your own if you were motivated to do so, but then you'd never be able to document what you learned. That's where official institutions really have a chokehold on the whole education thing. Universities and colleges have a monopoly on the credentials that prove what you know. They are licensed by the government as participants in a closed syndicate that controls the various forms of accreditation used to establish what people know and can do. All of that isn't meant to sound paranoid, but I guess it does. It's pretty creepy if you think about it. We all know how important a degree can be to your life; depending on your goals and aspirations, it can literally make or break your dreams. And a closed circle of established institutions controls the whole scene. It's an open conspiracy but a real one nonetheless.

> Universities and colleges have a monopoly on the credentials that prove what you know. They are licensed by the government as participants in a closed syndicate.

The Conspiracy of Accreditation

I'm going to return to journalism as an example and present a hypothetical situation. Let's say some guy named Bob knows a lot about writing and journalism, and wants to start a school teaching the subject. There is nothing that I know of to stop him. So he starts a school called Bob's School of Journalism, and he enrolls some students, and begins teaching them in his home. Now what's the obvious problem here?

None of Bob's students are going to get jobs! And why should they? When one of Bob's graduates goes to a media publisher, asks for a job, and lists her diploma from Bob's school on her resumé, she is probably going to get laughed at. But let's think about this for a moment. What if Bob really knows his stuff? What if Bob employs some other teachers who know their stuff? What if his students are as well or better qualified to be journalists, at the end of his program, than the average graduate from a college or university? Then a media publisher would probably be well advised to hire Bob's students. But it still won't, because it has no way of knowing that Bob's students are any good. And here is where we get the conspiracy of accreditation. It's a conspiracy upheld by government and the academic establishment, with the willing and enthusiastic support of private enterprise. It determines, either directly or indirectly, what kinds of qualifications are considered legitimate, and what kinds of qualifications are not.

In practical terms, the legitimacy of any college or university comes from government certification. If we extend some credit to the government and assume they are doing their job here, then the certification depends on certain minimum standards. Any institution that wants to award college diplomas or university degrees must meet these standards; the government monitors their compliance. But the fact remains that only certain institutions, and only certain *types* of institutions, can fulfill these requirements. This results, among other things, in a pretty narrow idea of what constitutes a decent education.[4]

Government involvement in the regulation of post-secondary education came along haphazardly and a history of how that happened deserves a book of its own, but the question of why it happened is fairly obvious. As education became more and more important to our complex modern economy, regulation was virtually inevitable. Government has always played an active role in matters that affect the economy. And so now they provide a check on which institutions can call themselves colleges and universities, and who can issue a degree or diploma. Students and parents shopping around for education no doubt find this very useful, but primarily it's a service that government performs for the business community, so that employers are able to properly evaluate the qualifications of prospective employees.

As education became more and more important to our complex modern economy, regulation was virtually inevitable.

It is interesting to note that even though our entire system of grading is a form of accreditation, employers are notoriously lazy about how much attention they pay to this information. Very

frequently employers look at the name of the degree and maybe the school it came from, but that's about all.[5] The university degree of a student who spent four or more years just scraping by looks just as good on paper as the degree of a student who did spectacularly well, and when they go hunting for jobs their degrees will be treated equally. If employers were really interested, they could pay attention to grades and course selection, but they choose not to. This laziness on the part of employers serves what I call the "Educational Arms Race" because the major distinction between doing well and just getting by becomes whether or not the student can continue to get a further degree or qualification. Unless the good student continues, however, the qualifications on paper don't distinguish the good student from the merely adequate student in any way employers seem willing to acknowledge.

Education versus Accreditation

Different people have different educational goals. Sometimes you hear people say they "learned nothing" in university. I hope if you take some time to think about your goals, you'll never have to say that, even though you might say, "I wasn't exactly learning what my program claimed I was learning." But if we're going to focus on what you want to learn and what you might benefit from learning, we've got to get over the idea that just because you are passing all your exams, or even getting A's, this somehow proves you are on track. It proves nothing of the sort. The whole system of evaluation is actually a pretty big distraction from many of the goals students have, and it certainly isn't required for learning. Depending on your goals, good grades might be a solid indication that you are heading in the right direction, but they certainly don't tell the whole story.

Evaluation is about testing what you know. Okay, some students would never be motivated to learn a damn thing if not for the fear of failing a test, but this is just confusing cause and effect. Entirely aside from any fear you may have of failing your next exam, let's assume you are motivated to learn. If you're going to learn anyway, then the process of testing what you actually know is just time you are wasting when you could be learning something else. Even worse than that, the test could be badly designed and end up testing not what you've learned in the course, but rather what you knew already, or even just a natural talent you may have for writing coherent essays, or for deciphering multiple-choice options. Quite a lot of evaluations aren't about checking on your progress, they're just another form of aptitude testing. Maybe aptitude testing is a critical part of moving further with education, which is where we get the GMAT, LSAT, and all the other -AT (Aptitude Tests) from, but does it need to be combined with your actual education?[6] I'd suggest not, and that in fact, it tends to get in the way of education more often than not.

I always tell students who aren't happy with their grades to look beyond the results they don't like — to demand tangible feedback.

There is a place for well-designed forms of evaluation, of course, if only to help students know if they're on track or not. The pressure to grade, however, and continually evaluate students to separate the good from the average from the poor, often dictates that quality feedback is lacking. You get your grade and not a lot else. I always tell students who aren't happy with their grades to look beyond the results they don't like — to demand tangible feedback on their essays, assignments, and tests, so they know how to improve for next time. When resources are stretched, detailed feedback is, sadly, sometimes not a priority for graders and instructors. And students who are excessively focused on the number at the bottom of the page learn to stop asking.

It's often the students who rely entirely on their grades and exams to indicate if they are doing well who will later say that university was either a waste of their time or else wasn't what it could've been or should've been. Well, there's obviously a problem there. If you spend four years looking at grades that say everything is fine, and then conclude it wasn't after all, it must be clear the grades by themselves aren't any indication that things are going well. Look beyond the grades and question your goals.

When Things Go Wrong

Let's face it, things don't always go the way we might wish. Maybe it's that first kiss with teeth bumping together instead of sparks flying, or the first car that you park around the corner rather than admit you own, or the first job that comes with a polyester uniform when you were hoping for your own office. We're all familiar with stuff like that. Well, university is no different. You might have a rocky start. In fact, allowing for how the experience gets built up and hyped, chances are very strong not everything is going to live up to your hopes and expectations.

It's one thing when the university experience as a whole just seems lacking. Most of this book is about how to overcome that, so hopefully you find some good advice on that topic. It's another thing when you feel as though you're letting yourself down, and not accomplishing what you've set out to accomplish or meeting whatever standard you expect from yourself. This experience can't be separated neatly from the problem of feeling let down by university, but it's still a different kind of problem. When you're in a place where you feel like your entire future is riding on your performance, and it just isn't coming together, that can be pretty awful. Never mind trying to explain that to the family.

Depending on your expectations, there's no easy answer or guaranteed system that will help you meet them. Not everyone is going to get into medical school, or law school, and no book can change that. But you'll probably do better if you can at least take some of the pressure off your shoulders, and there are some things you can do to help yourself.

Talk About It Early

If you've already started university and run into any kind of difficulty, this advice may come a little late, but one of the most important things I can say if you are just beginning your university career is: sit down right away with your family and talk about the fact that things might occasionally go wrong. The best time to do this is right around September because the conversation is obviously hypothetical. Parents and other family members don't like talking about the possibility that their children won't do wonderfully in university, but it's far easier to have that conversation in the abstract. Discuss the idea (painful though it may seem) that you might not get straight A's. Your university probably has some official literature on this subject to illustrate how grades change in university. Pick up some pamphlets from the Academic Advising office, and give them to your family. Even if you don't believe what's in them, and you still think you're going to be the exception to every rule, it will take the pressure off if you can convince your family to stop expecting miracles. That way it's a nice surprise if you're still the genius they always thought you were, and not a disaster if you turn out to be merely human.

You're going to know far more about what's going on with your education than your parents, so if you need to drop a course or make other tough decisions, they're going to have to trust you. It can be hard to convince family who went to university several decades ago that your reality isn't the same as theirs. It can sometimes be even harder to have that conversation if you're one of the first in your family to attend university but they still insist they know what's best for you. Talking about this in advance will make it far easier if the day should ever come when there is a real problem.

Some of the best students have to drop a course once in a while, or cut their losses in a program that isn't working out, or admit they simply aren't good at something. Your family wants to be supportive, no doubt, but it's in everyone's best interest to help them be supportive in a realistic way. If you're stuck in a situation where you're having problems in school and your family absolutely insists (from a position of total ignorance) that you've only got to "buckle down and try harder," that is simply not what you need. It might be true, at times, that you just have to work harder. It also might be the case that you've got to get out of a bad situation while you still can. And in order to make the best decisions, you need informed and sober advice, not blind faith.

If you're having problems in school and your family isn't aware of them, it's still a good idea to have this conversation, even if it comes a little late. The last thing you need is the added pressure of lying to your family. Even if you've successfully convinced yourself that things are going to be different in the future, there's no way to really know that. You're only burdened with the same assumptions of extraordinary success, and on top of that, you've got a history of not achieving it. Your chances of turning things around only get worse, not better, when you hide the problems you're experiencing. These conversations obviously aren't easy, and they only get harder the longer you avoid them. If your family really wants to be supportive, they'll understand. Your parents still love you even if you can't hit a fastball or play violin. The same principle really should extend to calculus.

There are some family situations, sadly, in which children just can't talk productively or safely with their parents on difficult topics. If that sounds like you, then you'll have to make up your own mind about what to say or not say. It is your life, after all. Remember that the university cannot and will not release any information to your parents, so you do have a measure of control. If your parents are in the

> The last thing you need is the added pressure of lying to your family.

habit of opening your mail (which is illegal, by the way[7]) get it sent elsewhere. It's an unfortunate option, but it's there, at least. Hopefully your parents and family can form an important support network. That's certainly the ideal, anyway. So involve them early, and honestly, if you can.

If you need some support and you can't talk with your most immediate family, definitely try to find at least someone to confide in and hopefully to get some advice from. This might mean distant relatives, it might simply mean friends and classmates, or it might mean university advisors employed for exactly this reason. Don't discount the value of talking with university counsellors, or feel as though turning to them for help is some sort of failure. They are knowledgeable about the campus, they've heard just about anything you might tell them many times before, and their only responsibilities are toward you and the university itself, so there's never any concern what you say will get back to the people you don't want to involve in your life. There's a lot to be said for all that.

Dropping Courses

Many students get through high school without ever dropping a course. Even when students fall behind, at that level, they can usually find options. Teachers might agree to accept assignments late, or assign bonus work, or allow other opportunities to recover. University is not so forgiving, and even sympathetic professors have little flexibility. Dropping classes in university is no longer a sign of failure, but a vital academic strategy used by even the best students. Get used to that idea now. It might save your grade point average one day.

Institutional standards vary, but at some point there's going to be a deadline beyond which you can no longer drop a course. Know when that date is approaching, so you can evaluate your progress. If you honestly think you aren't going to be able to pull up your grades in a particular course to the point where you're satisfied with them, you should drop the course. Or at least think seriously about it, and talk with academic advisors.

Dropping a course could have many implications and you've got to be careful. If you fall below a certain course load, you might have the government loan people mad at you, or else you could endanger a scholarship, or fail to meet the requirements of a specific program of study. There are many hypotheticals here, which is why I can't give you an exact rule to follow. But among the last things you need to worry about are what your parents will think, or what it says about you as a student, or even the loss of tuition. The last issue might be important to you, if you're really strapped for cash, but please don't let the loss of the course fee stop you from dropping a class if you think you should. Your education is a big investment, no question, but dropping a class at the right time might actually be the right move to protect that investment if it takes a poor grade off your transcript that would mar an otherwise good record.

> Your education is a big investment, no question, but dropping a class at the right time might actually be the right move to protect that investment.

If you are considering dropping a course, you might want to discuss the situation with your professor. University isn't forgiving, as I've said, so you aren't likely to be offered an assignment for extra credit or anything nearly so simple. But if you've got an essay outstanding and you want your grade back early so you can make a more informed decision, that's probably something your professor will accommodate. He might also be able to give you some sense of your standing relative to the rest of the class, so that if the grades are likely to climb, you'll know to expect that. Don't submit absolutely to the advice you receive, however, because your professor may be uncomfortable with the feeling he has driven a student out of his class, and could be just as susceptible as anyone to the illusion that you will simply "buckle down" and improve. Advice is good, but you're still the best judge of your situation.

As a final note of caution, please remember that standards of achievement are relative. I really can't say this enough. If you are literally failing a course, that's a good reason for anyone to drop it. No question there. But if you're heading for a C? For many students, that grade is perfectly normal, and there's nothing at all wrong with it. Someone, after all, has got to get the average grades. If you are used to A's, however, and you are heading toward a C in a course that just isn't coming together for you, that's a perfectly good reason to drop it. But you can't go around dropping every class just because you aren't an A student and wish you were. You've got to peg your expectations to your usual performance. If a class is going substantially worse than normal for you, that's a good time to start thinking about how to get out of it.

Rethinking Program Choices

It's one thing to realize that a course isn't going too well. Dropping that course might be tough, but it doesn't require you to rethink everything. Maybe it's something you don't need to take anyway, in which case the calendar is full of other options. Or if it is a required course you can always hope to do better next time, with more preparation and attention. But if you get to the point where you aren't doing well at most of what you're required to take, or else find that you're really not enjoying it at all and it's a chore to even pay attention in every class, that's a larger problem. Now you're re-evaluating some of the biggest decisions you made when you first applied to university.

First the good news. As a general rule, Canadian universities are structured so that you don't need to commit right away to any firm program direction.

You may feel as though you've committed to a particular program because you're already in it, or else have the idea that you've got to stay in a specific area because that's where you applied, but it isn't true. University is far more flexible about this than many students believe. It's easy to change programs. Many students make at least some sort of change in direction along the road to graduation. Systems vary between different universities, but in order to graduate, you'll complete an overall number of credits as well as the requirements for one or more program areas. Program requirements are designed, quite deliberately, to allow you to rethink your choices, and explore other options. Even if you totally switch directions at the end of your first year, you should have room, within your total credit requirements, so that you don't need to take any more courses than students who stuck with their first intentions.

If you thought you knew what you wanted to study, but grabbed a few electives along the way and discovered that some other subject is far more interesting, then you've got it fairly easy. It's great you've found something you like, so go for it. You may be concerned if you don't see any practical application for this area of study (something I'll discuss later), but at least you have a direction to follow, which puts you ahead of many students. It's a lot harder if you discover, at the end of your first year, that you simply don't enjoy — or aren't any good at — what you always imagined you would study. Then you've got a lot of thinking to do.

Switching programs can be difficult because it involves a lot of identity issues. Students often envision and plan their entire futures around program choices, and it's really tough to let go of those career plans. Forget about explaining to Mom or Dad, for a moment, that their smart little girl isn't going to be an accountant after all. It's hard enough to explain something like that to yourself. No matter what attracts you to a field in the first place, whether good reasons or bad, it feels nice to have some direction and it's hard to let go of it. But it's better to admit you're in the wrong area sooner rather than later, no matter how late it may already seem. Some people don't figure out they're in the wrong field until they've been working five or ten years. Think how bad it is then!

University programs tend to leave a lot of room for electives, especially in first year, so that you can explore multiple areas of interest. You should take this opportunity so that you have options, and other paths to follow, if your first idea doesn't pan out. And if you reach the point where you are picking first-year courses and you still don't really know what you want to study, it's nice to know you aren't stuck with your best guess, and you have some room to maneuver. It's really quite hard to screw up by picking the wrong direction in university, at least at the beginning. Even to the end of your second year, the system is surprisingly flexible.

Inevitably there are high-demand programs with tighter requirements than most, and special admissions procedures. If you applied to one directly from high school, you might find your requirements are more structured than other students' in first year, but you can still back out of the program. Getting into these "limited" programs can be a lot harder' than getting out, so it's true your options will be a little narrower at the end of your first year if you're shopping for a new program, but there's nothing at all wrong with the general programs. The tighter, more structured programs tend to be directed at very specific career goals, and unless you're sure that's what you want, you're probably better off with something broad.

If you're really sure you've discovered what you want to do, and you need to get into a limited program in order to do it, you should ask about that as soon as possible to figure out the requirements. It's still a competitive world and you may face an uphill climb, but if you really want to do something, then hopefully you have the drive to do it well. You may find you've passed the best opportunity to get into a particular area, and this can be discouraging, but examine all your options to see what it will take to get where you want to be. If you find this involves backtracking, or extra time in school, you may feel you've "wasted" your time in other areas, but no experience that leads to a firm sense of purpose is really wasted.

Trying Harder

When you've had a bad year, or a bad term, or even a bad week, it can seem like a pretty huge chore to turn things around. And you know, if it feels like a lot of work, that's probably a good thing. Because it is a lot of work. It's called "attending school full time" because studying properly, if you've got a full course load, is assumed to take up at least as much time as a full-time job. And if you slack off from that amount of work, it's only going to build up.

Don't get me wrong, it's very possible to recover from a poor start and still make the most of university. Some of the best students out there had a bumpy patch or two. But please don't just say to yourself that next time you'll "try harder." It's exactly that kind of attitude that causes problems in the first place, and perpetuates them.

Full-time study is not a short-term commitment. You can't just grit your teeth and try to get through it.

Full-time study is not a short-term commitment. You can't just grit your teeth and try to get through it. That works about as well as a crash diet. If you want to be more fit, you've got to change your lifestyle, not just starve yourself for a while. And if you want to succeed more in school, you've got to modify your lifestyle for that too. It isn't enough to just want it. You'll have to change things about the way you live, study, and prioritize.

I can't give you a magic formula that will motivate you more than you've been in the past. I think it's very important to know why you are in school and to focus on your goals, so if you're going to spend some time wondering how you can do better, those are good questions to address. While you're waiting for the next big revelation, however, you can take some concrete and manageable steps to improve. Check out some of the seminars designed to help with your study habits. I can't tell you where they're happening, but I promise every campus has them. Keep a Daytimer where you record how you're actually spending your time, so you can look at your week when it's over and see where it's all going. Form a study group. Record your lectures and listen to them on the bus. Try going to bed an hour earlier each night and see if it helps. It's amazing what a good night's sleep can accomplish.

Look, your Academic Advising office (which may have a different name depending on your school) undoubtedly has piles of literature filled with exactly this kind of advice, so I'm not going to repeat it all. Most of it is common sense and there's no use insulting you. You already know things need to change, and you probably have a good idea of how. Try something new. If that doesn't work, try something else. The important thing is to continue *trying*. As long as you are taking enough interest in your education that you're really working at it, things can't go far wrong. Just whatever you do, don't fall into the trap of resolving to "try harder," as though that decision alone is the answer to everything. It's the start, perhaps, but it needs to be accompanied by some positive change and concrete action. Then, perhaps, things will be different next time around.

Probation and Suspension

Different schools will have different systems for dealing with students who simply aren't performing to minimum requirements, but a few things are pretty much standard. If you aren't passing your courses, or are doing so poorly that you aren't heading toward graduation, you'll get a warning of some sort, and will (sooner or later) be placed on probation. That may come with some consequences, which you should pay attention to. If things don't improve, you'll be suspended. I know that's a very scary thing to talk about, but better to know now rather than later what it's all about and what it means.

Students who have just come out of high school

often have some pretty set ideas about what it means
to be "suspended," or even put on "probation." It's
a punishment, right? Usually for something like
fighting in the halls, cutting classes, or breaking other
rules. Well, it means something very different to be
suspended or put on probation in university. The
university doesn't really care if you show up to class
except if it affects your grades — and if you're
fighting in the halls, you'll simply end up talking with
the police. It is *possible* to get suspended for non-
academic reasons, but I'm going to assume you're
smart enough to not break the law on campus. The
vast majority of the time when you hear about
suspension at university, it's academic suspension.

So here's what it means. If you aren't performing
at a level that will allow you to graduate, the
university is going to warn you — that's probation —

and if you don't turn things around, you'll be forced to take a break — that's suspension. That's all. It probably feels like a kick in the teeth when you get a letter like that, but it isn't meant as a punishment. In fact for some students, it's the best thing in the world anyone can do for them. If you're only bashing your head into a wall, hurting yourself, and not getting anywhere, then someone eventually has got to make you stop. And that's what the university is doing when it suspends students. It's tough, but it isn't meant to be cruel.

Hopefully you won't face this situation at all. But if you run into problems at university, please keep in mind that you don't have to wait for the automatic mechanisms to kick in and force you to take a break, and to re-evaluate things. You can do that on your own. You can take some time off before the university suspends you, and forces you to take that time off. Then, when you're ready, you can take another crack at your studies. If you can identify the problems sooner rather than later, and take a break before you run out of chances entirely, you can avoid digging a deeper hole for yourself.

You Never Stop Wondering

So I know I keep talking about the need to know what you really want to do, and why you want to do it. It's true, you need some goals and aspirations to motivate you, and sometimes the ones you have (like the fancy car you want to one day own) just aren't cutting it. But you can also take this advice too far. Sometimes people get paralyzed by their inability to really know. It isn't just students, and it isn't just university. People have mid-life crises, and decide they don't like their careers anymore. They panic before they are about to get married, and sometimes back out. They agonize over decisions about retirement, and whether they really want to move down south. Second-guessing your goals and priorities is a part of life, and it never really stops.

If it takes some of the pressure off, try to remember that you don't need to know what you want to do with the rest of your life. It's important to at least have some goals to motivate you, but if they're short-term goals or leave some questions unanswered, that's perfectly fine too. Anyone who claims otherwise is full of crap. Turn the question back on them, and ask if they knew, even five or ten years ago, exactly how their lives would look today. No one ever knows. You never stop trying to figure out what you want to do with the rest of your life, and it's never too late to come up with some new answers to that question.

> It's important to have some goals, but if they're short-term goals or leave questions unanswered, that's perfectly fine too.

When things go wrong, all you can do is re-evaluate what you're doing and why. Take advantage of all the sources of advice that are available to you, and be prepared to make some tough choices. It's never easy to cut your losses and admit you screwed up, made a bad decision, or simply changed your mind. But everyone — absolutely everyone — has got to do it once in a while. The really successful people in life, the ones you are probably looking to emulate, didn't get where they are by never making any mistakes. It's how you respond to those challenges and unexpected turns that will make all the difference, so don't kill yourself trying to be one hundred percent sure at all times. It'll only interfere with your ability to rethink things later.

What Comes Next?

So at the end of the university rainbow you've got your education (hopefully), and you've got your degree. Congratulations! Your white picket fence, suburban semi-detached home, suv, and choice of dog or cat will be delivered shortly. Or not. We all know it doesn't work that way, but exactly how does it work? You're supposed to go out into the world and "be successful," but what will that really mean?

For many students, the degree is the goal. Getting the degree represents success in university, and it's what will get you a good job afterwards. The next challenge is to be successful in the workforce, and that's a whole new ball game. It's easy to fall into this pattern of thought, where the content of your education is only directed toward *getting* the job. But of course that isn't the only important thing. It's also about learning how to actually be good at something. As students compete for entry-level positions that don't seem to require any of what they've learned at university, this idea can be lost sometimes, but I've got to assume you want a job where you use what you know — at least eventually.

In a time when most waiters and fast-food managers seem to have degrees or diplomas on their resumés, it's easy to understand why people start to think the education part doesn't matter. If you don't actually need what the degree represents, then why do you need the degree at all? Why demand these qualifications for jobs that don't require them? The answer is both simple and sobering. It takes a degree or a diploma to get hired to wait tables because people with degrees and diplomas apply for those jobs. Between a university graduate and a high-school graduate, the university graduate will generally win. So if there are enough university graduates applying for the job, then high-school students are trumped out of the market, even if the job is only waiting tables. The problem perpetuates itself, and creates a competitive cycle of increasing qualifications. It's worthwhile to consider this phenomenon, and to know what you're dealing with, but don't get suckered into the mindset that only your degree matters — not what you learn. You may take some surprising turns in your working life, and end up doing things you may not have expected. Don't wilfully ignore the opportunity to learn while you have it. You'll only be limiting your opportunities.

The Educational Arms Race

People like to point out how complex our society has become as justification for the amount of education it takes to get into any kind of professional work. Does it really require four years of higher education to navigate a modern office environment and use the fax machine and photocopier? Or is it just that students are staying in school longer and the competition factor for the same limited field of jobs has driven qualifications through the roof? There may be a bit of the former, but I think there's a lot more of the latter.

Teenagers graduate from high school and look around at the prospects available. Work in retail and fast food isn't very attractive, so they stay in school if they can. I'm generalizing, but there's truth to this, and whether it happens on a conscious or subconscious level doesn't really matter. There simply aren't enough real jobs available for high-school graduates because college and university grads are applying for those positions. Some years later, those same students from high school, now mostly in their twenties and in debt, graduate from colleges and universities to go through the same process again. Some of them still aren't happy with the job prospects available and, if the option is there for them, continue on to graduate programs or professional schools. Many of the others snap up those entry-level jobs the high-school grads can't get anymore. Others go on to brilliant careers, and that's great, but it's still true that a lot of university and college graduates end up waiting tables and managing chain restaurants. That's partly because those who have two and three degrees scoop up all the better jobs.

Education becomes a kind of endurance test, where whoever can keep pace longest eventually "wins." It isn't really about what it takes to do the job anymore; it's about being more qualified — or more overqualified — than the other applicants. It extends into graduate programs, post-graduate programs, and to every level of education. It even influences academia itself. Time was you could get hired as a university professor with a Ph.D. and perhaps a couple of published articles, or even with a master's degree under the right circumstances. Now it often takes a post-doctoral program or two, and maybe a book under your belt.

The implications of this situation are manyfold, but for those less interested in theory and more interested in their own futures, there are still basically two options after undergraduate university, and they're the same two options that each and every person keeps coming around to. You can take what you've got and brave it out there in the "real world" of work, jobs, and bosses, or you can take another spin at the wheel and continue with education, at least assuming you have the grades and the financial resources to do so. Well, the undergraduate degree is at least a foot in the door. It's as good a time as any to enter the workforce, as long as you are honest about your situation. You've got the chance to make what you want of it, but your bachelor's degree isn't going to walk you straight into a job. And I think by now most of us know this pretty well.

Further Education

Around about the time students face graduation, the same problems come up again. For those able to continue on to graduate or professional school, it seems like an awfully comfortable idea because it answers a lot of those nagging questions, like "What the hell do I do now?" For many people, staying in school is a perfectly good answer, but beware of falling into that answer just because it's convenient, and seems to solve a lot of complex questions. Even more than your undergraduate education, the opportunity to pursue graduate or professional studies will be there when you are ready for it.

A general truth about education is that the higher you climb, the harder it gets to go back and rewrite past mistakes. You can drop out of high school, write some qualification tests at twenty-one or whatever, take a couple of night courses, get into an undergraduate program, and continue on as if nothing happened. We all know that's possible, and some people from that background are very successful. You can even, with a lot of effort, rebound from a mediocre undergraduate performance, and find your way into a decent master's program somewhere where you'll have the chance to prove yourself again. But that's about the limit of the flexibility in the system. If you go on to a professional school or a graduate program without being ready, and you drop the ball, you probably aren't going to get a second chance.

For all the same reasons that it's important to know why you are going into undergraduate university, it's that much more important to know why you are going further. If the door is open now, it should stay open in the future, at least until such time as you walk through and screw it up.

For all the same reasons that it's important to know why you are going into undergraduate university, it's that much more important to know why you are going further.

Many people continue education later in life. The age range among students at the graduate and professional level is quite wide. So be sure it's what you want and that your motives are sound — terror of the "real" world is a bad motive — or give yourself a year or three to sort things out. Taking your time is a good investment in getting these decisions right.

If you are interested in attending graduate or professional school, by the way, and you think you might want to continue immediately, you should start to seriously explore your options during the second-last year of your current degree. That will give you time to consider your options carefully, rather than succumbing to the sudden pressure of looming deadlines. With applications to prepare, funding to apply for, perhaps standardized tests to write, you'll find important deadlines are catching up to you even in September of your last academic year. Don't be caught napping.

Additional Training

Something that's becoming popular, as a form of additional qualification, is some kind of extra vocational training aimed at making a university education marketable and practical. More and more college programs are aimed specifically at those with bachelor's degrees but few professional skills. These programs are usually a year long, perhaps only eight months, and are designed to supplement a general arts or science degree. And really, it isn't a bad combination. The idea must have at least something going for it, because more and more universities are getting together with local colleges to offer joint programs that combine the merits of an undergraduate education with a college diploma.

Now, I think it's symptomatic of larger problems that we can't clearly separate the function of a college and a university. But if you are in a situation where you've just graduated from university, still don't have a clue what you want to do, and need some skills, it's a route you might want to consider. Far too many students graduating from university think they're too good for college. They're willing to consider additional education, but not if it's there. That's one prejudice we could do without. This entire book is aimed at the problem that everything seems to be called "university" now. That's bad because you don't know what you are getting. Well, colleges promise job skills. If you want those, then go to college, and be thankful you'll know exactly what you are doing, and what you are getting for a change. You might even find it refreshing.

1 In practice, there is no clear dichotomy between teaching faculty and research faculty. Different institutions place differing demands on their professors with either heavier or lighter teaching loads based on institutional policies and available resources. Professors who must teach more, inevitably research less, and so different classes of faculty have always existed. What is new, however, is a trend toward hiring permanent faculty with an explicit teaching role within universities focused otherwise on research, creating what many see as a two-tier hierarchy.

2 Institutional policies on grade distribution can be extremely hard to nail down. They aren't publicized because they are so subject to misinterpretation. Even those who properly understand the intent can find the information discouraging. They may exist only in the realm of convention or in guidelines issued to instructors. The one thing that remains constant is that your grades come from the department itself, and no instructor has unilateral authority to give you whatever grade he feels like. The department will always find some way to avoid aberrations in the system and major departures from what would be considered a normal class distribution of grades. Anything else would be unfair to students.

3 From the University of Toronto Scarborough Calendar. These courses perennially attract comments in student evaluations disavowing the idea that they are in any way easy courses, as warning to future students. Every year at least some students seem to make the same mistake anyway.

4 As colleges and universities are primarily a provincial matter in Canada, the precise relationship will vary province to province, but in Ontario, for example, the phrasing is pretty clear. *The Post-Secondary Education Choice and Excellence Act, 2000* reads as follows: "No person shall directly or indirectly do any of the following things unless the person is authorized to do it by an Act of the Assembly or by the Minister under this Act: 1. Grant a degree. 2. Provide a program or part of a program of post-secondary study leading to a degree to be conferred by a person inside or outside Ontario." I'm sure every province has similar legislation. The point is that it's an exclusive designation controlled by the government.

5 I'm not aware of any systematic studies into the question of how often employers request full transcripts from applicants or pay attention to their grades. Anecdotal evidence suggests that habits vary widely between different professional fields. In any event, the attention given to grades is inconsistent at best.

6 The GMAT (Graduate Management Admissions Test) and LSAT (Law School Admission Test) are standardized examinations required for application to the relevant graduate or professional programs in the United States. Some Canadian programs have followed this pattern; most notably all Canadian law programs require the LSAT. Though testing of this sort is less prevalent in Canada, it is used extensively in the States, and every student who wishes to attend college writes the SAT Reasoning Test — a set of standardized, multiple-choice exams.

7 In the *Canada Post Corporation Act*, it is defined as an indictable offense for anyone, including your parents, to interfere with or to open your mail. This is punishable by up to five years' imprisonment. In practical terms, of course this would never happen, but it's a fun fact to share with anyone who is in the habit of assuming that letters with your name on them are their business too.

GETTING MORE OF WHAT *YOU* WANT

What You Can't Control

University is quite the conflicted institution. It's full of all kinds of people running around trying to accomplish all kinds of different things. You can approach this as a big problem and think of university as a house divided against itself, or you can just accept this as the normal state of affairs in most large institutions. Either way, the important thing is to realize that it isn't dedicated to a single coherent goal.

A car wash is a place that's dedicated to one goal. Once you start at one end, you know exactly what's going to happen before you come out the other end. The place exists to clean your car, and that's what happens. A shopping mall seems to be dedicated to one goal also, but of course it isn't really. You can think of it as "a place to shop," but by saying that, you are assuming a degree of shared purpose that doesn't really exist. People go to malls for different reasons: some are looking for shoes, some are looking for a new stereo, and some are just looking to hang out for a while. When you walk in through the front doors, there's no guarantee about what you are going to come out with. A university, in this case, is far more like a shopping mall than a car wash. If you don't know why you are there, and you figure just walking in the front doors is enough to get what you want, you are going to be extremely disappointed. You can generalize and say that university is "a place to learn," but the statement is as inaccurate as assuming everyone goes to the mall for the same reason. People show up at university with different goals and for different reasons.

Perhaps the single worst thing about university is the way it often feels as though the other people around you are ruining your experience. The complaints that students have about other students are so numerous, it's almost pointless to list them. They never seem to end. *Why won't those idiots in the library shut up so I can study? What's wrong with all these people who act as though nothing is worth learning unless it can get them a job? Why won't that guy who answers all the questions stop talking so I don't look so stupid? Why aren't these people taking their studies more seriously? It's insulting to be around people who act as though this doesn't matter! Why are those other students taking their studies so seriously? It's impossible to get anything out of this experience if I have to study all the time just to keep up with obsessed people … .*

> Perhaps the single worst thing about university is the way it often feels as though the other people around you are ruining your experience.

It's fun, and often therapeutic, to just unload on the students who seem to be ruining university for you, but everyone is paying a lot of money to be there. None of them are paying it just for the pleasure of screwing up your life. Everyone has a reason to be in university, and if you find some people frustrating because they don't seem to have the "right" reasons, then chances are they think you don't have the "right" reasons either. You may have good cause to be upset when people around you seem to be throwing away their opportunities and interfering

with yours, but remember that everyone sees those opportunities differently. The real problems hit when you are thrown into the same environment with people who aren't out to get the same things you want, and the whole system is structured in a way that doesn't acknowledge this. So you have to fill in the blanks for yourself. You can't just do what everyone else is doing and hope it works out.

If it helps, keep it in mind that no one person or

set of priorities "owns" the idea of what university should be. If some people are there because they really love learning, then that's one aspect of university. If some people are there because they want good jobs, then that's another. Everything that's going on at university is valid at least to the extent that you can't fault other students for showing up to get something if the university claims to provide it. Of course there's a natural tendency to exaggerate the importance of what you personally want. If you can, look at the whole thing and realize that your purpose is no more and no less valid than anyone else's. That might at least cut down on the frustration factor.

So what's to be done? Well, the one bit of good news is with all these different things going on, there are at least aspects of university tailored to your personal goals. Whatever you arrived at university hoping to find, there are other people who agree with you — other students with similar goals — and people working in the system who are there to help you. If you know what you want, you can identify your allies and focus on what matters. That's the real trick. You have to be proactive in seeking out what you want.

I'll run through the five "types" I identified before, pointing out especially important aspects of university and making suggestions for each. These types are only examples for reference. They aren't neatly differentiated boxes, and not everyone will fit into one exclusive category or another. Take what you find helpful from each, and chances are you'll find at least something of use in each description.

The Academic Student

So you showed up at university because you just wanted to learn. You opened up the calendar and you couldn't even decide where to begin. So many courses and not nearly enough time! You were looking forward to a place where everyone was serious about learning and people would stop goofing off all the time. You were eager for a chance to follow your interests instead of constantly studying what you were told to study. And you wanted to really learn from and interact with experts in their fields. So what happened?

You found a school that's even more faceless than high school. You found that the students around you might be a little more engaged than the bottom-line average you just left, but that isn't saying much. You were able to drop some of the subjects you don't care about, but when it comes to learning things that you do care about, you are still fed the same general program of what's "good for you" rather than what you find most interesting. The "benefit" of learning from experts and university-level professors is that you generally don't get to see any of them, making you feel even less engaged than you did in high school. Where's that community of scholars you expected to find? Isn't this supposed to be where the real education starts?

Well, as I said, there's no blanket solution that will create an institution filled with people who share only your priorities. The bad news is that a lot of the students you'll meet at university simply won't approach education the same way you do. The good news is there's still a real undercurrent in academia that supports your ideals. Most professional academics (professors) got into the field because they feel this way themselves. Connecting better with faculty will go a long way toward finding the more academic education you are looking for.

Some Basic Ground Rules

Professors are human. This may come as news, but they're just like anyone else. Dealing with them involves some common sense rules that apply to many other interactions in your life too. Treat them in an appropriate adult way, and you'll receive the same in return. If you still think of yourself as a kid in some sense, just do your best to fake it, but keep in mind that they won't make allowances for you on that basis. University assumes you are an adult and so do your professors.

Your professors' opinions of you (when they hold them at all) will be affected by all your actions. If you act like a fool in class, talk during lectures, and fall asleep with your head on the desk, they will have an understandably low opinion of you no matter how good your work may be. If you ask questions you could easily answer yourself by simply reading the syllabus or your course calendar, they will think you're lazy — and they'll be right. They won't care if you wake up one day and suddenly decide you want to be serious, and they won't bother to distinguish between the personality you exhibit when you want to be taken seriously, and the person you are at other times.

More and more interaction takes place over the Internet, and this is a particularly dangerous area where students allow all kinds of bad habits to creep into their interactions with professors and other university figures. If you send e-mail from hot_ monkey_love@hotmail.com, with poor spelling and grammar throughout, you are going to look like an idiot. So get a respectable e-mail address (you almost certainly have one through your school), and proof-read (at least quickly) before you click "send." Don't lace your e-mails with Net shorthand, and don't insist that your professors get back to you "ASAP." I know at least one professor who will not only take longer to reply, just to annoy you, but who will definitely hold it against you in the future. It bugs him enough that I've sat through a monologue on the subject. And really, it is kind of obnoxious. Between friends is one thing, but unless you are good friends with the professor in question, it just seems demanding.

When you make a bad impression, it *will* come back to haunt you. You may think it's unfair for your professors to hold past actions against you, but really it's only human to do so. I judge people by their past actions, I assume you do too, so why wouldn't they? Hopefully it won't affect the way they grade your essays, though don't count on it one hundred percent if you've really annoyed them. It's definitely going to affect the way they think of you if you ever want something special — such as an extension on an assignment, or a letter of reference — and you never know when that might happen. Remain at least reasonably mature and professional at all times and you won't have problems down the road.

When you make a bad impression, it *will* come back to haunt you.

Incidentally, you may be tempted sometimes to think your professors aren't so smart after all. Either the content in your lectures seems a little basic, or you get into an argument in class and a professor backs away from it, or they generally just seem unimpressive in conversation ... it can be tempting to imagine that's all there is to them. I wouldn't blame you because I used to think the same myself. And then I got into the same argument *outside* of class and had my ass handed to me. Remember that the classroom environment, and professors' undeniable role as service providers, puts certain limitations on them. What you may see on the surface isn't all there is.

Different Kinds of Faculty

For your purposes especially, not all faculty are created equal. The folks you see at the front of the classroom are a mix of full-time professors, instructors on short-term contracts (essentially academic "temps"), and occasionally graduate students who are picking up a bit of work to get through their own schooling. This was covered in detail in Chapter Two. Sometimes it can be hard to differentiate between instructors because they all seem to be doing more or less the same thing, but there are some very important differences in terms of how they'll interact with your life at university. So it's a good idea to learn how to tell them apart from one another.

Professors with tenure form the real backbone of any faculty. These are full-time academics employed to instruct undergraduate-level classes, certainly, but they are also expected to conduct research, probably offer graduate classes (if there's a graduate program), and collectively perform all the administrative functions that are necessary to run their various departments. Sometimes you will also encounter "pre-tenure" professors who are progressing toward tenure and are employed on more or less the same basis. The only difference is that they are still within an evaluation period that lasts around five to seven years. In Canada, the large majority of pre-tenure faculty ends up receiving tenure.[1] It's these tenure and pre-tenure members of faculty that you really want to connect with.

Now, before I seem to dismiss the instructors on temporary contract unfairly, I'd like to point out that they may be great instructors and highly qualified in their particular fields. As I said, some are graduate students, and others may be recently graduated academics just picking up work where they can get it while hoping to land more secure jobs. As you might imagine, there are only so many permanent jobs available for scholars of Victorian-era literature in any year (or any other specific field of study), and sometimes even great young scholars have to work for a few years as temps. But here are the limitations. First, these are temporary positions; while they may be extended on a year-by-year basis, there's no guarantee they will be. So you may build a relationship with someone one year, and find them gone the next. Second, individuals in these positions are not expected to have anything to do with the administration of the university (in contrast to tenured faculty, who essentially *are* the administration of the university). As a result temporary professors frequently don't have a clue what's going on outside of their lesson plans. Third, they have no motivation or obligation to do anything other than show up for their lectures, keep a few office hours, attend to questions, and grade your work. And that's all that most of them ever do. Finally, while you might hope that a really good temp or sessional instructor might win a job as tenured faculty at your institution, that very rarely happens. Unlike an office environment where a temp worker might get a full-time job, the hiring practices to find and retain permanent faculty versus temporary instructors are so completely different that it's a long shot at best.

Recognizing who is and isn't tenured (or pre-tenure) can be tricky. A good place to start is your course calendar. Often calendars are printed before temporary instructors are hired, so if a particular professor is listed there, it's a good sign. Also, most universities follow a convention of hierarchy that moves from assistant professor (junior) to associate professor (journeyman) to "full" professor (senior). Anyone noted as an associate professor, or just simply as a professor, is almost certainly tenured. Assistant professors may be either pre-tenure or temporary. Sometimes you will see people noted as instructors, lecturers, or something similar, and those are usually designations given to sessional or temporary instructors, though some universities are moving toward systems that afford a bit more job security to professional lecturers. Other good places to find out about these things are department websites, as they often have very comprehensive lists of faculty and sometimes longer descriptions that may include how long they've been with the university, past administrative appointments, awards won, etc. Anyone with a history will immediately stand out, and you'll know they are obviously tenure-stream.

If you are really in doubt, and you want to know who has a continuing appointment and who doesn't, it isn't the worst thing in the world to simply ask. Better yet, ask some other professor who you are sure is tenure-stream in the same department. The distinction is very important in the academic world, and professors themselves have a way of drawing this line, so if you want to know, even as an under-graduate student, it isn't unreasonable. Be polite, obviously, but you might find that just asking the question engages the interest of your professors and instructors because so many students don't realize there's a difference at all. Even if you ask someone who isn't tenure-stream, it could lead to some interesting opportunities. If your instructor is a graduate student, you could ask about his or her thesis. Graduate students are almost always willing to talk about their theses. Alternatively if your instructor is an academic looking for work, you might be interested to know where he or she eventually ends up. The point is that it isn't an inherently rude topic to ask about.

Apart from other practical considerations, and the potential that any particular "temp" might be a really good instructor, it's probably in your best interest to avoid them as much as possible, especially when you start to look at senior-level courses in your later years. First, best intentions entirely aside, the hiring policies and practices to find and retain these instructors are always far less stringent than those for tenured faculty. Sometimes sessionals are hired based on no more than a read through a stack of resumés.

The process to hire tenured faculty, in contrast, can take a year or more. So while individual cases may vary, your odds of getting really good instruction from permanent members of faculty are higher. Second, if you are really interested in learning, then chances are you might be interested in graduate school, or may decide later that you are. The additional benefit of learning from tenured faculty is that they very often have reputations in their respective fields, and when you apply to graduate programs, their names will carry some clout. While not all tenured faculty have notable reputations, it's virtually certain that graduate student instructors and sessionals have no reputations to speak of.

One other type of professor you might encounter is the professor emeritus. Though perhaps you haven't met one, you'll see a number of them noted in most lists of faculty (the plural is professors emeriti). The title is largely honorary. When a professor retires, in many instances, he becomes a professor emeritus and will be listed among the faculty for as long as he lives. Once in a while, you might see professor emerita used instead, as a feminine alternative of the title. This practice is an extension of the university principle that holds that a member of faculty is a member for life. Sometimes professors emeriti will offer courses even though they are technically retired. They may be retired because of mandatory retirement rules, or perhaps because they wished to reduce their commitments but didn't want to leave entirely; in any case they do occasionally offer courses, and if you have the opportunity to take one, it's probably a good move. You might be afraid that you're signing up for

lectures from some doddering old fool who hasn't
been qualified to teach for a decade but actually there
are probably stronger controls on the quality of these
professors than others nearing retirement. Because of
tenure, it frequently isn't possible to remove a
member of faculty from the classroom until they've
retired, even if they aren't as solid as they once were,
but once they are actually retired (as in this case),
there's no obligation to let them come back and offer
courses. So if that's happening, you can have some
confidence that they are still on their game. Also, you
are sure to get someone who genuinely *wants* to
teach. On top of that, you are learning from someone
with a real reputation, built over a lifetime, and good
enough, if nothing else, to earn the title of emeritus.
Point being, if you get a chance, taking a course or
two offered by a professor emeritus is probably a
very good idea.

A final category of professor has several variants in usage such as distinguished professor, university professor, or similar. Some universities award this special title to a very small fraction of faculty to recognize outstanding reputation and scholarly achievement. If you encounter the term among your professors, it certainly identifies a scholar of high standing and someone to keep your eye on.

So now that you know how to identify the various types of faculty, let's talk about how you can get more out of the system by engaging with them.

Their Research and Your Independent Study

As you near the end of your degree, you might find you want to do some kind of independent study. Remember how annoying it is that you still can't learn about the things that interest you most? Well, there is almost certain to be some option available to you to engage in independent study. But in order to do that, you'll need to find an appropriate member of faculty to supervise your work. This can be tough because professors aren't paid extra, and don't really get credit for doing this other than an occasional pat on the back. You definitely want to ask a permanent member of faculty for this supervision, because temp instructors have no reason at all to add work to their load, and in many cases might not even be allowed to. If you want to engage in independent study, it's incredibly helpful if you've already developed some kind of relationship with a professor or two. Then you'll know whom to ask. It's also very important to ask someone whose field relates to the area you want to explore, which is one reason you want to know something about your professors' research interests.

It's easy to imagine that what professors do outside the classroom has no bearing on the average student. Well, probably it doesn't have much bearing on the average student, but that doesn't have to include you. Find out what your professors are researching! Hit the academic databases and run their names if you are really curious. You might be surprised at what you learn. Even just a random search on the Internet could turn up a lot. At least try to know their general areas because that way you'll know who to approach with your own interests. Maybe it feels a little pretentious to go investigating your professors' publications, but at the university level it's time to get over the feeling that showing some initiative is a form of overachievement. I guarantee that all the faculty members of your department are aware of the sorts of research their colleagues are engaged in, so why shouldn't you be too? You might find it interesting.

> It's time to get over the feeling that showing some initiative is a form of overachievement.

Sometimes your department will invite visiting professors to give lectures, or perhaps your university might host a conference related to your area of study. If your department is searching for a new tenure-stream member of faculty, there may be several lectures offered by candidates as a sort of in-class trial. This may seem obvious, but go! The education you receive in the classroom, simply by following the syllabus and your course outlines, is limited by necessity. In order to get at the kind of education you really want, you are sometimes going to have to go outside of the classroom. You'll also find that very few undergraduate students jump at this sort of opportunity, so merely by attending these events, you'll distinguish yourself and have an opportunity to interact with professors you may not know yet, and also meet the few other students who share your degree of interest. This creates opportunities for later.

Overcoming the Intimidation Factor

All of these suggestions, as I'm sure you've noticed, rest on the assumption that you aren't intimidated by professors, and that you are willing and able to approach and communicate with them. I know that isn't always easy. All I can do to make it easier is remind you that professors are just students who have been at it longer. In the same way that we can all learn new things even from people who have less formal education than we do, professors can and do learn from their students all the time, and are interested in doing so. If you find you share any areas of common interest, the fact that you are less qualified as a scholar doesn't make your conversation any less interesting to them. And most especially, as professional scholars, your professors aren't necessarily any more comfortable in social settings than you are. Some are natural extroverts, of course, while others may find it painful on a daily basis to get up in front of a class. So make the effort, even if it's difficult, because if you don't reach out to them, it will be far too easy to blend into the background of the lecture hall for years at a stretch. At the very least, start by visiting during their office hours, and asking some of the questions that occur to you in class. And if a group of students seems to be hanging around for a few minutes after class to ask questions or continue discussion, join the group, even if only to listen.

There is always a fine line between interest in a professor and simply chasing her around and abusing her hospitality. Students are sometimes worried about this, and sometimes that worry is justified. Most professors are professional enough that they won't clearly tell you to go away and leave them alone, but they may occasionally wish to. There's no sure way to gauge every social interaction with your professors any more than it's possible to be sure where you stand in other social contexts. So just feel your way as best you can. Keep in mind that your professors don't necessarily regard your company as work all of the time and might actually find you interesting. Also keep in mind they might not. If you find you are having trouble figuring out your relationship with a particular professor and deciphering his "signals," the best thing to do is ask one or more students who seem to have a good relationship with him for their advice.

Beyond all of these suggestions about getting more in touch with faculty and the work they do, there are bound to be opportunities available to exceptional students to do things that most students simply don't do. There are undergraduate research journals designed to give you a chance to publish. There are research conferences you might attend where you may even present something. There are chances to get involved with your professors' research, and perhaps get credit in connection with one of their publications. But all of this is non-standard stuff. It isn't something that will be brought to the attention of your entire class or pitched to the average student. So if you want to know about these opportunities and to be considered for them, you first have to make sure your professors know who you are and realize that you are serious about your education.

After University

If you are the kind of student who just loves what you are studying, it's possible you haven't got many concrete ideas about where you are heading. Graduate school is the obvious choice because then you get to keep learning and, if you're good, you can even get it funded so you can stop paying out of pocket or accumulating debt.[2] Getting to know the right members of faculty is going to help you immensely if that's the path you want to follow. Once you start talking about graduate programs, the various fields of expertise have narrowed enough that all the really reputable people know one another. You want to get into cross-cultural psychology? Everyone really working in that area is aware of everyone else. French Renaissance literature? Same situation. When it comes time to apply to graduate schools, you'll want the advice of the most appropriate members of faculty, because not all graduate programs are created equal. It isn't just a matter of picking the right school. A particular school might be great in some areas and very mediocre in others. And if you're looking at a Ph.D. program, finding the right thesis supervisor will be key, and could easily affect your destination. You'll want lots of advice about where to apply based on your interests, and you'll definitely want strong letters of reference.

Letters of reference are one of the biggest areas that students screw up. Again, professional scholarship is all about reputation. When you apply to graduate school, you are going to want at least two or three strong letters of reference, and you want them to be from acknowledged and successful scholars. There may be only one real expert in a particular sub-field at your university, but your other letters should still come from reputable professors. Don't ask graduate students. Don't ask teaching assistants. Don't ask sessional instructors unless you really think you'll get a far better letter. Don't ask university administrators. This is why you build relationships with the members of faculty who will still be there when you graduate four years later, over and above every other benefit. You want letters from the right people, and you want them to actually know something about you so their letters don't come across as cold and mechanical. Even more than that, the world of academia is small enough that it's entirely possible there may be a personal word or two exchanged about your application at a professional conference or someplace similar. And this sort of thing can go a long way.

This is a good time to note the value of keeping records and files of the work you've done. You might be nearly best friends with your professor, but after four years, she isn't going to remember what you wrote in her first-year class. In order for her to compose an informed letter of reference, bring your old work (the good stuff) with you when you speak to her about that letter. You might also want to refer to your past work when considering your future direction, or you might find the seed of an independent study in something you did years ago. So if you're serious about your studies, make an effort to keep track of the work you've done.

Moving on after university can be strange, terrifying, and exhilarating, especially if you aren't interested in graduate school right now, but love learning, and aren't sure what you want to do with it yet. I hope you aren't in debt after your very expensive education, because there are only so many things you can do in this world while trying to pay down a student debt. If you managed to stay debt free, you can go wherever you want, do whatever you feel like, and continue your education in whatever way seems best to you. That kind of education doesn't require letters of reference or formal applications, and who knows, maybe you'll produce the next *Walden*. But if you want to do something different with your life, don't write off your professors as a source of ideas, inspiration, and possible introductions. They may all seem awfully old, settled, and middle-class to you, but believe it or not, most of them went through a questioning phase also, and you'd be amazed what they might turn you onto, if you listen.

The Vocational Student

Okay, so you know what kind of career you want. You've come to university because you want an education that will allow you to get the job you want, and live the life you envision. Fair enough.

What you found is a school that seems to spend an awful lot of time forcing you to learn things you don't imagine you'll ever need. You wish there were more obvious connections with the job market and with potential employers. You worry about the eroding market value of your very expensive education. You wonder how you'll ever be able to distinguish yourself in the working world with your degree when it seems as though absolutely everyone is going to university today. What went wrong?

The most important thing to acknowledge is that the competitive market value of an undergraduate university degree is, unquestionably, eroding. As more and more people receive at least some education at the post-secondary level, the distinction gained from that education must inevitably shrink. But there's no sense being bitter about it. The only thing to do is figure out how to achieve whatever success you are aiming for regardless.

Substance versus Flash

Career-minded students are very conscious of their credentials. Well, credentials are good. But it's important to know the difference between credentials that matter — those that reflect real learning — and those that don't. Students sometimes get funny ideas about the importance of certain kinds of credentials. In the interest of hauling in another line for the resumé, they sacrifice opportunities to develop tangible skills. Don't get me wrong, an impressive-looking resumé is always nice, but in the end you'll do far better with skills and abilities you can actually demonstrate.

First, let's talk programs of study. What do you have to do to fulfill your degree? Generally speaking, there are your basic requirements to graduate (complete X credits), and then there's a mess of other requirements relating to majors, minors, and areas of specialization. Often students seem to think they can gain additional qualifications by grabbing extra minors and double- and triple-majoring. While those efforts are admirable, it shows just how far education has departed from a focus on learning students imagine that the title of a program is more important than the content of its courses.

Here's a basic truth. Programs of study are assembled using approximation and guesswork. A major in economics at one university doesn't look exactly the same as a major in economics at another university. Why? Because each of these programs was put together by a different team of professional academics based on their assessment of what it takes to do graduate work in economics, or else to enter the workforce and work in business, or else to add some other professional certification and begin a similar career. They design the program around the general goals of the students who are most likely to enroll in it. Opinions differ on exactly what kinds of skills are most vital to achieve these goals, so programs differ as they reflect one opinion or another. But the line on the transcript, "major in economics," remains the same. In any case, it represents the sum total of the various skills you learn in the classes you're required to take in order to complete the major. It doesn't mean any more or any less. The content of the education is in the courses you take, not in the number, or the impressiveness, of the titles used to describe them.

The content of the education is in the courses you take, not in the titles used to describe them.

Program requirements will change over time. Maybe the industry, or the field of study, has evolved.

Maybe the program is simply influenced by new professors with new ideas. Either way, there's no absolute, concrete definition of what a major or a minor in any particular field must include. Not only are the requirements fluid, they are also the result of broad generalizations. The academics who put these programs together don't know exactly what you want to do with your major in economics; they have a more general idea of what most students probably want to do with a major in that area. I'm sure it's obvious that a one-size-fits-all approach to education isn't the best you can do. You can pull your education off the rack, if you want, and just take what you are supposed to take in order to complete your program. With a little more effort, however, you can also get an education that's tailored to your personal goals and aspirations. And I promise it's going to fit better.

Concentrate on the courses you select, and look beyond the titles of both course and program. Sit down with whatever kind of academic advisors are available to you. Sit down with career counsellors. You pay for these services, so take advantage of them. Discuss your goals and ask for their advice regarding what courses you should be taking. You might be amazed at the sorts of suggestions you get, because the one-size-fits-all approach really leaves a lot out. If you are interested in sales, you might be directed entirely outside of your subject area and advised to take a few courses in media studies. Maybe you are interested in motivational speaking and life coaching, and you'll be sent over to learn some psychology. Don't discount these suggestions! These are more important than any line item on your resumé or transcript. Make sure you select your courses in a way that fulfills your need to graduate, but beyond that requirement, your only other consideration should be building the skills that will allow you to follow whatever career interests you.

That said, it's probably obvious by now that there isn't much of an edge to be found in just a university degree. Like it or not, just or unjust, the job market out there is demanding more, so it's a very good idea to look for ways to distinguish yourself. Of course universities are aware of this also, so they are competing with one another to repackage their product in a way that will make it more attractive and competitive. But this is one of those times when you need to work extra hard to distinguish between product and packaging.

Universities are competing with one another to repackage their product in a way that will make it more attractive.

One thing universities have been doing lately is offering more and more interdisciplinary programs. They're pretty easy to spot. If it seems as though a program is obviously drawing in courses from different academic areas, and especially if the program doesn't seem to own a course code of its own, then it's interdisciplinary. These programs are like any others, except that they are trying to anticipate the sort of thinking I've already outlined. Let's say the people running an existing commerce program notice there's a big demand for media-savvy people in sales. They get together with the folks in media studies, stick some courses together, and come up with something called a "Major Program in Commercial Media." Sounds impressive, doesn't it? Well, I just made it up. And so do they.

I don't want to run down interdisciplinary

programs in general because some of them are very good, but I want to illustrate two things. First, you can get similar benefits simply by identifying your own career goals and by branching out into complementary areas of study. And second, universities are very motivated to repackage their product in a way that makes it look special when it may not be. A well-developed interdisciplinary program is a wonderful thing, but one done on the cheap can be worse than any plain old everyday program. If you are looking at an interdisciplinary program and it has its own identity, some kind of supervisor or co-ordinator exclusively responsible for it, some core courses unique to the program, and it offers something truly distinctive, then that's great. Chances are it's a quality program. If, however, the program consists almost exclusively of courses from different disciplines, doesn't seem to offer anything unique or particular, and doesn't boast any faculty associated primarily with that program, then there's a very good chance it's all presentation and no substance. It's just empty credentialism, and this time it's being sold to you directly by the university itself. Isn't that aggravating? I know it annoys me. So evaluate your program options carefully. You are far better off in a standard program run properly than in a slapped-together assortment of courses with no direction or focus.

Other trends in education connect a university education with directed job skills. These are often called joint, concurrent, and direct-entry programs.

Other trends in education relate to a desire to connect the status of a university education with some directed job skills. These are often called joint, concurrent, and direct-entry programs. Generally speaking, these are quality programs because they involve multiple institutions and/or administrative units, and no one wants to put their name to something if the other partner isn't upholding their end of things. The common element in all these programs is that you apply just to the undergraduate university; once you're accepted, you move through two programs at the same time and emerge with multiple qualifications, or else you finish one program, then are immediately guaranteed entry to the next.

Joint programs at the undergraduate level are typically arrangements made with colleges, so that you graduate with both an undergraduate degree and a college diploma, usually with a specific career focus. Concurrent programs allow you to pursue multiple university degrees as part of a combined program of study, often shaving a year off your total time in school in the process. Direct-entry programs are arrangements made with professional schools and second-entry programs, so that you graduate with an undergraduate degree and a professional degree. As these programs tend to be small and tailor-made to suit partnerships, there's no way to make sweeping statements that will cover them all. If your university has these programs, they may well require application directly out of high school. If you're already at university and still interested, you should seek out the program co-ordinator(s) to ask about your options.

Joint, concurrent, and direct-entry programs are indicative of the changing nature of education. People are looking for guarantees. In the case of direct-entry programs, it's awfully nice — if some kind of professional school is your goal — to know that you are sure to get in as long as you maintain a clear standard of performance. Of course everyone else can apply to the same schools after graduation, but in a direct-entry program you know exactly what you need to get in. As more and more colleges offer programs tailored to university graduates designed to add marketable job skills to otherwise general undergraduate degrees, it only makes sense for colleges and universities to combine forces. These innovations respond to demands made by both the job market and by students. An undergraduate degree, on its own, isn't all that special anymore. Of course there's still a lot you can do to improve your prospects without signing on for more education.

Mentorship and Networking

One of the key things to look for is a mentorship program of some sort. If you attend an established school, and especially if you are in a vocational area of study, then chances are very good there may be some kind of mentorship program that will connect you with people working professionally in your field. Universities habitually invite their alumni to participate in programs of this nature. Ask about mentorship programs and opportunities — ask student organizations, ask your department office, ask your Office of Advancement (the folks who stay in touch with alumni to work them for donations and commitments). If you find your institution doesn't have a mentorship program at all, offer to help start one. That's a hell of a lot more work than just signing up for the program, but I promise that the benefits you'll gain from helping to found such a program will outweigh the extra time and effort you'll put in. You may never even get a mentor, but the connections you'll make in the process of helping to establish the program will be gold.

Talk to career counsellors, your professors, and program supervisors, and ask about ways to get more out of your program. We all know that volunteering and community involvement is good, that's a given. Volunteering at a hospital looks good on your resumé because it demonstrates you are a decent person. But unless you're actually interested in a career somehow related to health care, you need to get more precise with your efforts. If you are going to volunteer your time, make sure you are doing it in areas that will feed into your education and professional goals. Ask about those opportunities. And again, if the programs don't exist, then offer to help create them. It sounds like a lot of work, and it is a lot of work, but if it's what you want to do with your life then that should make it interesting, and a little easier to handle.

If you are intrigued by business, government, the not-for-profit sector, or teaching, do not neglect the university itself as a source of professional experience. Universities are fascinating institutions because they touch on so many different areas, and because opportunities for students to get involved in what goes on there are virtually endless. Universities have committees for just about everything and almost all of them need student involvement. If you aren't sure where to start, then ask around. Ask your department office and any professors you know. Ask other involved students. Your students' union (or council or whatever) is a good place to find out about opportunities, and don't neglect that as a source of experience either. Many student organizations are incorporated, have boards and jobs they need to fill, and offer all kinds of opportunities to gain experience. Definitely don't make the mistake of confusing student life at university with what you know from high school. When student organizations start to make decisions with implications in the hundreds of thousands of dollars, it's obviously real business. And future employers know that.

After University

If you plan to directly enter into the workforce after graduation, then your time at university is especially important for building networks. If there are opportunities to shore up your marketability with professional designations or other qualifications, then you should definitely take them. At the end of your undergraduate degree, as you open up the paper and start leafing through the classifieds, your goal should be to have much more going for you than just one more section on your resumé. That might be nothing more than the promise of a stellar reference from a university administrator whom you've worked with on and off for a couple of years, but don't underestimate the value of that reference. Employers will want to know what you did during those years at university, other than graduate with a degree to show for it.

If your goal is professional school, then letters of reference may count (depending on the area and the specific program), and connections might do you some good also. In contrast to letters of reference for graduate programs, professional schools don't exist in the sort of closed academic environment where everyone notable knows everyone else. For that reason, it's more important to produce truly glowing letters of reference, hopefully from people with important positions and titles, than it is to get them from professors who have reputations in their fields. Consider the range of applicants a teachers' college receives. They draw in students from literally every academic area. There's no way they can be aware of everyone's reputation when reading letters of reference, so get your letters from significant figures and make sure they are strong and personal, rather than ensuring they come from the most qualified academics.

Finally, if you are facing graduation and still don't feel adequately qualified or prepared for the workforce, do not discount the value of the right college diploma program to top off your university degree. One or two additional years of education aimed at practical, marketable skills is a more and more popular option; colleges are targeting this market. Definitely seek advice from career counsellors and other advisors, but don't be turned off by the idea that there's something undignified about going to college if you are already a university graduate. By following this path, you can acquire all the benefits of a joint program with the ability to choose exactly how, when, and where you do it.

Do not discount the value of the right college diploma program to top off your university degree.

The Certification Student

Your prospects right out of high school — social, economic, and otherwise — were downright scary. You knew you wanted more than what was available to you, and the decision to go to university made a lot of things easier. Your parents and family are happy with you and leave you alone; you have a perfectly good answer to give when people ask, "What are you doing?" (you're "going to school"); and most of the time you can convince yourself that your life is going in the right direction. So why do things feel so shaky and uncertain? You're doing everything right, so why don't you have faith in it?

If you're reading this book, you probably have the idea by now that a university degree isn't the ticket it once was. Sure it helps, and it's a necessary step for many people to get away from the sorts of jobs they don't want, but look at all the people around you in school. Many of them are heading toward the same degree as you, and you've got to think about competing with them for jobs when this is over. It could be like high school all over again, with thousands upon thousands of graduates streaming out of the universities and hitting the job market. Will you be able to find the kind of job you want, and live the kind of life you want, if all these other people are out there looking for the same thing? On top of everything else, you might not even be sure you're in the right program; it just seemed like the thing to do at the time.

Your instincts and concerns are more accurate than anything you've been hearing from your parents and family, or any message you've been fed by popular culture. Your parents aren't in university; you are. Their ideas of higher education were formed a generation ago when the reality was different; you are in the reality of today. You can stumble through three or four years of education and emerge with a degree, but if you have no plan beyond that you won't be in a good spot. The reality is awfully different from the image people seem to have of guaranteed success and unquestioned status, which they associate with the mere achievement of graduation.

The Economy of Motivation

Students who show up at university because it seems like the thing to do typically end up in the large "generalist" program areas: English, philosophy, psychology, biology, whatever. They aren't in the smaller, more directed programs. Now there's nothing wrong with the large programs at all, but consider who else is probably in these areas with you and sitting in the classes beside you. Students who want to get into law school typically take philosophy, political science, and English. Those aiming for teachers' college might be in any area. Every subject area also numbers students who just really like what they're studying. A truly remarkable number of students in first-year science courses are aiming to get into medical school. That's a problem itself, because most of them won't get in, but they're sure motivated to try. These large program areas, these "generalist" programs, are not filled with students who are just aiming to get through their education, but include many highly motivated students. And that's what you are competing against. /

Forget about the grading curve for a moment. Forget all that stuff about how much you should expect your grades to drop between high school and university, and what those grades really mean now, and all the rest of it. Think about this as a general question. If you are trying to do something, and you don't really care much about it aside from a feeling that it's what you are supposed to do, and you compete against people who are really motivated to do well, what's going to happen? It doesn't have to be university; it could be sports, politics, gambling, or anything else. If you set yourself up in a situation where you are competing against people who are significantly more motivated than you are, they are probably going to beat you. And that's what's happening at university, so long as your primary goal is simply to get through it and emerge with a degree. It doesn't mean you're less intelligent or less capable than anyone else, it just means you care less. But the odds are extremely strong that your grades are going to reflect this lack of motivation. And remember, this will limit your options when you are done.

If you are absolutely sure you only want to get through university, take your bachelor's degree, and enter the workforce, then your C average (or whatever) is perfectly okay. It will see you through your degree and keep you out of trouble. But the whole reason you're feeling a bit lost is that you aren't entirely sure what you want, right? What if you decide later you do want to be a teacher after all, and you need to stand your grades up against those people who approached their studies with this goal in mind? What if you decide you want to go further with your education? There are always ways to try to get back into the system, but don't lie to yourself now about how hard that will be. If you graduate with a degree that reflects a general lack of motivation without any real idea of what you want to do with it (other than "be successful"), you are stacking the deck against yourself in the future no matter what you finally decide. The only way your decisions will get easier is by process of elimination, as you narrow down your list of available options.

Locating a Goal

Now for the good news. Your university is filled with programs, departments, advisors, and opportunities that can help you find some reason to care about what you're doing. There's no right reason, and there's no simple answer. You just need to sit down and really think about (and maybe talk about) what you want out of life. Okay, I'll admit, I'm making it sound easier than it is, but it's still something that you need to do.

There are all kinds of people out in the workforce doing things that have no real relation to their degrees. Probably you've heard that before. Maybe it's part of what contributed to your idea that how you do in school doesn't much matter. Well, for some people, that's true, but you still don't end up in a career entirely by accident. Find something that interests you. It doesn't have to have any relation to what you are learning in class; it just needs to be something you care about. Volunteer for your campus radio station, coach a sports team, or get involved with some kind of community outreach program. It may seem counter-intuitive, but you'll do better in class just because you have a reason to show

up for school, even if it means putting some time into something that isn't academic. I can't draw a straight line to illustrate how coaching a university sports team helps you get to where you want to be in life, but people who care about what they are doing, and are engaged in their environments, are simply more successful. So if you really can't care about what you are doing in class, at least find something to care about outside of class.

If you think you might have an idea of the sort of career you want, but it's always been something just lurking in the back of your mind, then it's a really good idea to start looking at it directly. Universities are all about this stuff, so use the resources available to you. Visit your Academic Advising office, your career office, or whatever it's called, and start asking questions. If you're going to need more education to get where you want to be, you need to know that now. If you're going to need some kind of internship, you'll want to know that too. If you've been surfing along on the assumption that you'll go to graduate school or something, as a way of pushing back the question, then at least get a solid handle on what you'll need to get in there. Graduate programs are fiercely competitive, and you need to either compete at that level or be more self-honest about your goals.

The one other thing you can look at changing in order to find some greater motivation is what you're learning. If you've got no particular goal other than to graduate with a university degree, you've got an entire calendar full of courses you could be taking. So what interests you? If you really don't have an answer, so be it, but at least take some time to seriously ask the question. You don't need to stay locked into choices you made when you first applied if those choices no longer make sense.

The hardest part about approaching some of these questions is that you probably feel like you've been doing everything right, so you don't deserve to feel lost or concerned about your future. To a point it may be true that you've done everything you're supposed to. But the simple truth is that doing everything right is not necessarily enough. It's good enough for "okay," and that's what you'll get if you continue the way you have been. Your university degree will get you out of food service, front-line retail, and probably manufacturing (though some of those jobs pay pretty well), and will get you into the white-collar sector, but I suspect you want more than just a job that will keep your hands from getting dirty. And stimulating jobs, the kind you can really feel good about, aren't going to just fall in your lap.

So whether in university or outside of it, you're going to have to start thinking about what you really want. You've got to define what "success" means to you, and then care about it enough to work for it.

The Good Citizen

According to popular wisdom, university should be the best years of your life. That's certainly the message you are getting from parents and popular media, at any rate. You aren't entirely sure what that's supposed to mean, but you have faith this whole process will make you a better person in some indefinite way. You may not be the best student in the world, but you know you can handle the work just as long as it seems like it's actually going somewhere. But when you don't even know what you're waiting for, it can be a little hard to focus.

A whole lot of other people seem down on university and it's not easy to get inspired when everyone else seems lost. For a time that's supposed to be the best years of your life, there's not a lot going on. Actually the whole place seems kinda dead. The course work is manageable, but not especially interesting, and it's harder to handle now that you're feeling let down. And it's difficult to ignore the fact that you're paying an awful lot of money for this.

Well, I hate to repeat the old mantra about how you get out as much as you put in, but it's as true here as anywhere, and it's where the solution is going to start. Of course, when you are surrounded all day by interesting and intelligent people, the elements are all there to have some of the best times of your life.

Hopefully you have enough time to enjoy it. This feels like a good place to acknowledge that sometimes students are working their asses off to afford education and, as a result, end up with no time to enjoy or benefit from it fully. I hate the cost of education and the way in which that cost skews the whole system, but just this once I'm going to advocate for debt. Take whatever kinds of loans you can get in order to pay for your education rather than work all the time to support it. No full-time student should be working more than a dozen hours a week at absolute most. I know you sometimes can't avoid it, but if you can, do. Education isn't only about what happens in the classroom, and you don't just get it from books. You may be working so hard to pay for your education that you don't realize you're missing half of it.

> You may be working so hard to pay for your education that you don't realize you're missing half of it.

Education is awfully expensive these days, and that's having an impact. It isn't just you, it's also the students around you who are more serious, have less time to "waste," and are more committed to getting something marketable out of their education. Of course that statement makes certain value judgments you probably don't agree with, and I wouldn't encourage you to agree with. Social time is not "wasted" if it's directed toward something you care about. Learning about things you are interested in is not less valuable than learning career skills. And there are lots of things to get "serious" about other than the fastest and surest path to economic success and social standing. This aspect of university has been sleeping lately, but it isn't dead.

Connecting Education with What Matters to You

If you approach course selection in a way that's geared only toward satisfying program requirements, you've been lured into the same false perception regarding the importance of those programs (majors, minors, etc.) that career-driven and credential-minded students often fall into. As noted, those programs are only valuable to the extent that they reflect groupings of courses that will teach you certain things. The education is in the courses themselves. For a career-driven student, the obvious thing is to approach course selection from a personal perspective and to consider the skills that best suit his or her goals, rather than trust blindly to program design. Similarly, if you are trying to get something personal out of university, you can't assume you're going to get that simply by signing up for program X, taking all the things you are supposed to take, and all the things everyone else is taking. If you find the process a little disengaging, that should come as no surprise.

You may find your mind is frequently on what's going on outside of the classroom rather than what's inside. Isn't that a part of university too? Hell yes, of course it is, but the two are tied together in ways that aren't always obvious. You don't need to be in love with school but the goal, at least, is to find things that don't entirely turn you off. So same lesson as for career-driven students, except this time you are aiming to connect with your interests rather than with job skills. Electives are your friends.

Students often try to approach electives as a way to find "easy" courses, but for reasons I've already discussed, that's always going to fail. One student's elective is another student's program requirement, so there's nothing inherently easier about them. You've also got to assume that when some students walk into a classroom where they are learning things they care about and find interesting, and others walk in with no motivation aside from the hope that the material will be easy, it's pretty apparent who is set up for the fall. So skip worrying about easy for a moment. A course is easy when you're motivated to learn. Flip through the calendar and look for courses that seem like they'd actually be interesting to you. If the descriptions you find in the calendar aren't good enough to figure it out, ask other students for their opinions. Keep an eye out for dynamic instructors. If your school has an Anti-Calendar (which provides student feedback on courses and instructors), use it. Don't ask about what's easy. Ask about what people really enjoyed, why they enjoyed it, and then think about whether the same thing might work for you.

University may be more than just the books and the lectures, but that doesn't mean you can ignore them either. Lots of students get inspired by what they are learning, and take those ideas to their natural conclusions out in the real world. So take a chance on a wide range of courses. Don't neglect what you must do in order to graduate, but keep an open mind about changing programs if you find your required courses are a lot less interesting than what you take out of personal choice. Maybe you could rearrange things so that more of your electives contribute to graduation, and so you are able to take more of what you enjoy. If you aren't sure how, ask for help. That's what academic counsellors are for. You may find there is a little voice in the back of your mind that's nagging at you, keeping you in some program you don't really like because you are worried about your job prospects and future career after all. In the end, you've got to do what's right for you, but you should consider that you'll always be happier and more successful doing something you care about than something you are forced to do — even if you are forcing yourself. That is no less true out in the "real" world. It's easier to see how some subject areas might get you a job, sooner than others, but you aren't doing yourself any favours if you turn away from your natural interests just because you can't immediately see how you'll make money from them.

If you are really turned off and uninspired by some or all of your professors, try to remember that they haven't been hired because they are necessarily the best teachers out there. This is one of the ways in which the other priorities of university crowd in on what you want out of the experience. You'll never beat that system, but I can recommend two ways to approach it. First, some professors *will* be dynamic, interesting, and inspiring. Find a couple and get to know them. Of course you'll also discover these are the most popular professors (not surprisingly), and their time is at a premium. You'll probably also discover they are involved with interesting things, and know a lot of other students who have been attracted to them for the same reasons that you are. Once you are introduced to that circle of students, you might find you have interests and activities in common with them. Second, you never know when you might discover a hidden gem of a professor that other students don't know about. Even if your professor is dry as toast up in front of the class and puts everyone right to sleep, that doesn't mean she is as boring in person. Lots of people have trouble speaking in front of large crowds and your professors are no different. Take a moment to visit each of them at least once or twice. You never know what you might discover if you talk to them in person, even briefly, and the nice part about the less exciting professors is that they don't tend to attract the same following. As a result, you can usually get bigger pieces of their time.

Finding Life at School

Forget the classroom for now. You came to university to get inspired, and you may never care all that much about what's happening in your classes. You may find you're comfortable with that as long as the rest of the experience comes together. So what if you can't find life outside of the classroom, either? You may find university doesn't look or feel at all, in reality, the way it appears in all those television shows and movies you watched growing up. You may feel there should be more going on and yet somehow, there just isn't.

Well, the ugly truth about university is that it's just like anywhere else in life. If you wait for things to be handed to you, it just isn't going to happen. Similarly, the social environment at university isn't going to come right out and introduce itself to you. Yes, it takes a little bit of work, but that shouldn't be surprising because most of the social scene at university is created by other students anyway. Clubs, student societies, and other kinds of initiatives are all student-run. There isn't some teacher or professor lurking in the background, secretly running things while maintaining the illusion that students are in charge of their own stuff — it really is all done by students for students. That's both good and bad news for you. It's bad because at times things can be a bit disorganized, and since no one has the outright obligation to make anything happen for you, sometimes no one does. It's good because opportunities to do stuff and have a meaningful role in making things happen are almost endless.

What you are going to get a lot of, if you go around asking, "Why doesn't our university have *this*?" are invitations to go ahead and start whatever it is you are looking for. Don't take that personally, because you really can start your own club, initiative, or whatever. If you are up for it, then go right ahead. If you are just starting university and don't have a lot of established networks to draw on, however, you should probably start by getting involved with, and contributing to, what's already there.

There's no single formula for how to get involved in student life, but if you really can't find it, then you probably aren't looking. Go to your Office of Student Affairs (or whatever it's called, the university office that handles student stuff that isn't academic), and ask about clubs and how to contact student groups. Go to your students' union (or council, or whatever you have) and ask the same thing. These days you don't even have to do that personally if you don't feel like it because all the same information is almost sure to be on-line. Look it up. Then, once you are in touch with people who are interested in the same things you are, show up. What happens next is up to you.

The funny thing about the social environment at

any university is there's really no such thing as a bad
situation. If the social life of your campus is thriving
and it comes right up and hits you in the face
(although this almost never happens), then you've got
no cause to complain. And even if things are completely dead (again, almost never the case, really),
then you've got unlimited opportunities to do
something yourself and get the credit for starting it.
No matter what's going on, there will always be at
least some involved students who will tell you there's
plenty to do — and another group of students who
aren't doing anything and complain that the place is
barren. Talk to happy students from a large institution and they'll say they love being somewhere there's
a lot to do and where there's always something
happening. Talk to unhappy students from the same
place and they'll say they wish it were smaller and

more intimate so they'd know more people. Happy students at a small institution will praise the intimacy of their school, while the unhappy ones will wish it were larger so there'd be more to do. The lesson here? Everyone is in a hurry to either blame or credit the environment and the situation they are in, but really it all comes down to attitude. If you are doing stuff, you'll be happy. If you aren't, you'll be unhappy. So no matter how bad you think your university environment may be, you can always start doing something to fix it. Even if you end up accomplishing almost nothing in terms of doing more for the people around you, I promise you'll end up feeling better about things personally because you, at least, will be doing something. The success or failure of your initiatives may not even matter that much.

If you find you are really involved on campus but you are semi-enthusiastic, at best, about your studies, that can be okay, but you've got to manage your commitments and mindset in a way that gets the most out of both aspects of your university experience. Look for ways you can get credit for what you are doing extracurricularly. Some institutions will have a co-curricular transcript, which is an official record of what you are doing outside the classroom. There are always awards for student life and similar involvement; there might even be scholarships available that heavily consider such activities, though they probably have at least a minimum academic component as well. This is all good stuff for your resumé when you graduate. As mentioned, the undergraduate degree is now a foot in the door, no

> Look for ways you can get credit for what you are doing extracurricularly.

more and no less, so it's a good time to start thinking about what distinguishes you. Don't think of this as some kind of exercise in inventing false qualifications or resumé padding. Think of it as getting credit for the things you are doing anyway and really care about!

At Home on Campus

If you want to get the most from the whole university experience, it's important to live close to the action — in residence if possible, or perhaps just off campus. Of course not everyone can afford to start paying their own rent, and many students continue to live with parents and family while attending university. It should be near the top of your priority list to live as close to campus as possible, and that might even affect your choice of university. If you have to commute for an hour or more to school every day, in each direction, there's just no denying that it's going to affect your ability to be involved with campus life. You may tell yourself that it won't matter, that you'll still make the effort to get down to campus for everything you want to do, but there's obviously a disincentive. This also provides a rough way to judge the amount of life you are likely to find at a particular university. The greater the percentage of students living on campus, or right next door, the easier it is for everyone to just do more. It isn't an absolute rule, but if you're shopping for a university where a lot is going on, it's something you might pay some attention to.

Residence makes a good first step for anyone looking to leave home. It's convenient, usually guaranteed for at least your first year, and less complicated than looking for your own place. You may find, however, that you can find a better deal living off campus with a couple of roommates, and that's something you might want to look at in later years. Often a university campus will generate a fairly active rental market catering to the student clientele. Of course, if you move off campus, you've got to start dealing with landlords who might be looking for a year-long lease, utilities, phone, and cable, not to mention figuring out whose name they're going to be in, and the whole roommate thing in general. University residence cushions the full effect of having roommates by putting locks on your doors, treating your finances separately, and not holding you all accountable for each other's actions. If you sign a lease with a couple of friends, and one of them stops paying his share of the rent, the landlord isn't going to care which of you isn't coming through — you're all responsible. Oh, and the place probably won't be furnished for you. Just some stuff to keep in mind.

Fraternities and sororities are one other option, but if you're really looking for that experience in Canada, do your research well in advance. They simply don't have the same presence here as on U.S. campuses, and if you want to find one that suits you, it may involve choosing a university specifically for that reason. Don't expect to find a major recruiting drive on campus, or for their members to come right up and introduce themselves to you. It's something you'll have to look for.

If you just can't afford to leave home, look for ways to compensate for that. Join groups that are active on campus and make some friends. If things are running late, you can probably find someone who'll let you crash at their place overnight. Rules differ about these things, but it's something you should be able to get away with once in a while. Try to find a "home" on campus, whether it's the office of the school newspaper you write for, the women's centre where you volunteer, or somewhere else. It helps an awful lot to feel as though you have somewhere to go when you're at school, someplace to just sit and put your feet up where people know you. It's cliché but true, and especially important if you don't live on campus but expect to spend a lot of time there.

> Try to find a "home" on campus, whether it's the office of the school newspaper you write for, the women's centre where you volunteer, or somewhere else.

Staying Afloat

Watch for warning signs in your studies. You know yourself better than anyone, and I can't tell you exactly what your warning signs will look like, but if your work habits start to slip, that's a problem. If you aren't terribly interested in your course work, then nothing can change that, but if you start handing in your assignments late on a regular basis (that's just throwing away marks), or showing up to exams completely unprepared, then those are obviously bad signs. If you find you are prioritizing the extracurricular things you do on campus higher than your school work, and especially if you find yourself taking on more and more as a way of avoiding the school work, that's definitely a problem. For some people, and maybe you are one of them, the non-academic activities at university are the only things that get you out of bed in the morning and motivate you to show up. I would never advise you to stop doing what you care about. There has to be a balance, however, and only you can find it. Every campus has a few stories about the heavily involved students who seem to be doing everything except passing their courses. Every students' union has the anecdote about the president or executive who got suspended while in office ... too busy representing students to be one. Try not to be that story, okay?

If you get worried, every once in a while, about what happens after university, that's good. It's great to throw yourself into something, but it's also nice to have an idea of what you're going to do with yourself once it's over. Contrary to popular opinion among students, life doesn't really end at twenty-five or thirty. Also contrary to popular opinion, life does not automatically make more sense when you get older. So if your plan right now is to just do what you have to in order to pass, get your credits, get your degree, graduate, and get a job, then that's fine. Getting out of university with a degree takes more in the way of discipline and commitment than it does talent or interest. Sure, it takes both talent and interest to do really well, but to just get C's for three or four years? You can do it. Just about anyone who gets in can do it, otherwise they wouldn't get in.

After University

If you've been active in university for three or four years, you should graduate with something to show for it. Don't just accumulate line items on your resumé; work to maintain the contacts you've made. Think about what you really know versus what your university degree says you know. Maybe you don't care much about all the stuff you learned en route to your biology degree, and you immediately forgot most of what you memorized to pass your exams. But that recycling program you worked with on campus? You feel that was the most worthwhile thing you've ever done. So? The recycling industry employs people. Did you spend your time planning campus events, dealing with insurance, budgets, promoters, and all that stuff? Well, people get paid for that too. Get your references in order, and make sure that wherever you go afterward, you'll always be able to take credit for the experience.

In terms of your other options, just remember where you're going to be at the end of your degree if you keep getting those C's. If your goals require professional school, second-entry programs, or graduate studies, you are going to have to get a lot more serious than C's. Down the road, if it becomes important to you, you might be able to fight your way back into the system, but don't kid yourself about how easy that will be. Getting back into higher-level education with an undergraduate transcript that shows you did enough to pass, and no more, is far harder than getting into an undergraduate program when you haven't finished high school. You can jump through a whole lot of hoops to prove yourself, and it might work out in the end, but you'd have to really, really want it. And if you don't want it now when you've got the chance right in front of you, the odds of wanting it that much more down the road may not be great. So at least give it a think through and be sure of your priorities.

Of course all of this assumes that a certain degree of social and professional standing are among your goals in life, as well as a certain level of income.

Unfortunately, if you are going into debt for your education, that's something you are almost immediately forced to think about. If you have the luxury to graduate debt free, however, you can still do almost anything with your life whether it pays well or not. It isn't hard to live as a single adult on minimum wage working forty hours a week, if you are willing to make certain sacrifices, and devote the rest of your life to whatever you really care about. You can start that rock band, if you want, or write a novel and try to sell it, or join a commune somewhere. If that's the sort of thing that's ever crossed your mind, well, when you graduate from university in your twenties (presumably), you're pretty much able to do whatever you want. The only thing stopping you will be your other priorities. You can't have everything, after all. But it's also worth keeping in mind that your priorities may change down the road and you'll always have more options if you do well in university. All things being equal, keep those grades up if you can.

The Holding-Pen Student

If you ended up in university because it seemed like the thing to do, and it isn't even about what you want or don't want out of life, but is simply what's expected of you, then you're in for a rough ride. I know I keep talking about categories of students and types of purposes as though they are hard and fast definitions, but of course they aren't. Probably you want "to be successful" as much as anyone (isn't that what we all want?), but if you aren't even sure what standards you wish to follow and you're at university just because it's simpler to be there than not, you've gone beyond the problems encountered by those students who want a certain standard of material and social success, and simply don't know how to get it. You're in a whole different place. You're set up to fail, and if you ever sit down and think about it, I bet it pisses you off. It would sure piss me off.

First point. You aren't stupid. You've been fed assembly-line style into a system that's designed to measure you against other students. Quite a lot of them already know what they want (or close to it), and as a result they're working hard (or close to it), and you aren't. So you aren't doing particularly well. The system spits out grades that seem to indicate you're stupid when, in fact, you just don't particularly care enough to try. Probably you know

all this on some level and it helps you to ... well, to not care. You could do better if you wanted, but you just don't see why you should. That isn't really helping, is it? The whole "not caring" thing is the problem.

Students who don't actually want to be in university might end up there for any number of different reasons: family pressure, general apathy, the vague hope it might be less trouble than finding a job. The results are rarely good. It's no different than walking into a theatre when you don't want to see the movie, ordering a big meal at a restaurant when you aren't hungry, or going out on a date with someone you don't actually like. Everyone knows those things don't work out well. It might be a really good movie, and it might be your favourite meal, and someone else might really enjoy themselves on that date, but it doesn't change the fact that you were set up to have a bad experience from the start. And the worst part is that it doesn't just feel as though university has let you down. That movie, that meal, that date ... you can trace all those situations back and realize that at some stage you made a bad decision. Okay, you can deal with that. But going to university never felt like your decision in the first place. Your friends, your family, your teachers, your counsellors, and a whole society that has a kind of fetish for higher education pushed you into it as if you didn't have a choice. Of course you did, and you do have a choice, but that doesn't alter the feeling that the system let you down and made that choice for you.

Obviously it doesn't have to be like this. If you

A whole society that has a kind of fetish for higher education pushed you into it as if you didn't have a choice. Of course you did.

hear one more time that your university years are supposed to be the best years of your life, and it makes you want to scream, then something has got to give. You're young, and you've got choices and options in your life, and that's what makes these years good, not where you happen to spend them. It seems like any time people start talking about students who are having problems in school, there's this immediate defense that kicks in. School isn't just about the academic subjects, gaining job skills, and finding a career; it's about *life* skills and all of those lessons learned outside of the classroom! Well, here's a hint at something you probably picked up on a long time ago. Life skills are learned anywhere. They're called life skills because you learn them by living, not by being at university. And you probably learn them faster living downtown in a cheap apartment that you share with three friends, working at some stupid job to pay for it, than you do in the protected enclave we call university which, to be honest, very often bears little resemblance to real life as it exists anywhere else.

You Don't Have To

If you've been waiting for someone to say it, then I'll come right out and say it. If you don't want to be at university, then don't be. In fact, if you really don't want to be there, then you shouldn't be there, and the best decision you ever make might be to leave. If you don't know what to tell your parents, you can hand them this book and underline everything that makes sense to you. If you need someone to blame it on, you can blame it on me and they can send me hate mail. But if you're pissed at a system that let you down, then you deserve to be pissed, because any so-called "guidance counsellor" who was doing his job, and at all interested in guidance, should have told you ages ago that people don't belong in university if they have no reason to be there. It's a bloody expensive way to waste your time and screw up your options in life. Even aside from the time you are wasting, and the amount of stress and misery you are inflicting on yourself, let's look at where you are actually heading.

Your best-case scenario is that you keep it together for however many years it takes to graduate, you stay out of academic trouble, and you emerge with a degree. Congrats, you've probably beaten the odds. Now you'll have a degree to get your foot in the door, and you can look forward to a white-collar job you don't care about rather than a blue-collar job you don't care about. With an undergraduate degree that reflects all that time you spent not caring about your studies, you can pretty much write off any chance of going further with your education. Because you obviously aren't getting into graduate or professional schools with those grades.

Did I just say graduate or professional school? But right now I'm writing about students who don't even want to be in undergraduate programs! I'm talking to the students who are just scraping by and should be happy to get their degrees if they can; it isn't like going further was ever in the cards for this lot. Wrong. Refer to the first point. You aren't stupid. I don't have a clue what you want out of life, and maybe you don't either, but the fact that you lack motivation and don't care about education at this particular time doesn't mean you aren't suited for it. I'm not surprised you might feel that way after spending too long in a system that seems designed to send you exactly this message, but the system is flawed, not you. Maybe one day you'll know what you want, and maybe you'll find you need a graduate degree, or some kind of professional designation to get there, and that's just fine. All kinds of people find their careers and vocations in their mid to late twenties, thirties, or even later. I'm not saying that's necessarily an ideal life path to strive for, but who goes around defining these things anyway? Chances are that most of the people who've been feeding you ideas about what your life should look like never managed to follow that advice themselves, so what do they know?

There's only one way you can really screw up higher education and that's to go at the wrong time, with the wrong attitude, and either flunk out entirely or graduate with grades that simply won't allow you to do, in the future, what you may decide you want to do. Not going at all is hardly the worst-case scenario (no matter what your family might think) because that keeps all your options open. If you've got the grades to get into university now, you'll still have them later. If there are savings to support your education now, there will be savings later.[3] And if you have to go into debt to pay for it, well, you can do that later too.

If you've got the grades to get into university now, you'll still have them later.

If education were free, or far cheaper, it might be more reasonable to say to yourself (or to hear from other people), "Well, just give it a year more and if it still isn't working for you, maybe try something else for a while." But given the cost, you aren't just wasting your time, hacking away at subjects you don't care about, you're also going into significant debt, or burning your available resources, when realistically you were set up to fail from the first day you showed up. It's just awful when students who have no reason to be in higher education are convinced to go anyway. They may very well use the one financial opportunity they'll ever have. They may have such bad experiences, they'll never even consider going back. And they may be potentially good students who would succeed at some future time, when they have better reasons to be there.

If you're already in university and a lot of this is hitting home, then you've got to start making some choices and do what it takes to get your priorities straight. Is there anything going on in school you can

really get excited about, or do you just want some time to figure your life out? If you think there's still something you can get out of university, then go ahead and get it, but know what you are paying for that opportunity. There are always second chances in life, but they don't come cheap. If all you want is some time to figure things out, then you might really want to explain all that to whoever chased you into school in the first place. If it was just yourself, you've got it easy. If you have to explain to Mom and Dad, that might be harder. But at some point, you need to be honest both with yourself and with the people who care about you.

Time to figure out your life is the cheapest thing you could ever ask for. You don't need to pay thousands of dollars a year and go into debt for that. You can get some stupid job that comes with a low wage and minimal responsibilities, and spend all the rest of your time sorting out what you want from life. The great thing is you actually make money doing that, rather than accumulate debt. If that's what you want to do, then do it. But if you leave university without finishing, don't think of it as a failure, or at least don't think of it as *your* failure. You were tricked into playing a game you didn't care about in the first place, so it's hardly your fault if you've "lost." Keep that in mind, because you never know when you might be motivated to play again — on your own terms.

1 Tenure rates among pre-tenure faculty are internal information among universities, and I'm aware of no general study of retention rates in Canada. The University of Toronto, however, conducted an academic planning exercise in 2003 resulting in a "Green Paper" document that addressed this subject. The Green Paper notes U of T has a tenure rate of 95 percent of pre-tenure faculty, despite considerable emphasis on high standards. This document is hosted publicly on the Provost's website.

2 Funding available for graduate studies in academic disciplines (as opposed to professional graduate studies such as MBA programs) tends to be quite good, at least certainly compared to opportunities at the undergraduate level. There are many deadlines and complicated applications to deal with, however, so you should start exploring your options as early as possible. Seek advice from professors and the university services designed to help you.

3 Some savings plans may create complications, or impose direct or indirect penalties, if they aren't used for your education within a specific time frame. If you are facing a situation of this nature, you should investigate the details carefully. It's possible the person who has set aside savings for you does not entirely understand what happens if you don't immediately attend school, and may therefore put more pressure on you than is necessary (even with the best of intentions). Where significant incentives exist to compel you into post-secondary education sooner than you'd like, you have a difficult choice to make, though I still believe you are better off waiting even if it costs you more in the long run. Any savings plan structured to reduce the ability of students to pursue education when they are best prepared for it is awful, by the way. It should not be allowed.

CHAPTER FOUR

INTERNAL CONTRADICTIONS

Things That Don't Make Sense

As university tries to serve various competing interests and functions, it gives rise to a whole set of difficulties and contradictions. By occupying a position in society where it seeks to be the answer to everyone's "success," even though success so obviously means vastly different things to different people, the institution of university ends up in a trap where it's trying to do everything all at once for everyone.

I still believe it's possible to get what you want (or at least more of what you want) out of your education. It takes some personal initiative, and some insight into what's going on, but it's possible. One of the things that stands in the way of a lot of otherwise motivated students, however, is that the whole thing seems to make so little sense. So I'd like to address that feeling of aggravation. I can't make the contradictions go away, but explaining them, at least, seems to help a lot of people.

Grading

I have to open with the big one. Everyone gets excited about grading. Everyone has at least one secret beef with it, even if they don't say it out loud. We are graded on essays, tests, group work, and class participation. We write multiple-choice exams, long and short answers, and we fill in blanks and label things. We describe and remember things, make presentations and displays, and sweat through just about every kind of evaluation imaginable. In its various forms, all our work gets fed into the system, and it spits out results labelling us as good students, average students, poor students, and failures.

Some students are confident they understand how grading is supposed to work, but feel it goes wrong sometimes, rewarding or punishing the wrong people. Some consider it a naturally obscure process they aren't likely to understand anyway, and just hope to get through it with minimal pain and suffering. One thing that's certain about evaluation is that no one can afford to ignore it. It plays such a pivotal role in the lives and futures of every student. Whether you're aiming for a graduate program, or simply struggling to graduate from the one you're in, your grades are going to determine your fate. Maybe you've got family who are going to look at your results at the end of the year, and those grades will determine what they think of you. Maybe those grades will determine what you think of yourself.

There will be methods of evaluation that you hate. Sometimes you may feel the system is arbitrary or unfair, and sometimes that may even be true. Nevertheless, things work in predictable ways, and however you feel about testing, or particular forms of testing, you've got to play the game even if you don't like the rules. You will sometimes need to deal with methods of grading you don't agree with. You may dislike the concept of grading entirely, and feel as though chasing grades is a betrayal of your ideals. But you never know when you are going to need the grades to back up what you've learned, providing you with future opportunities.

A lot of this is common sense, but when you get a syllabus, actually look at the grading scheme. Figure out where the marks in your courses are coming from. If you've got a tutorial, and there's no grade attached, you can consider it optional if you really want to. But if it's worth 10 percent of your final grade to show up regularly and say something half intelligent, then it's not really optional anymore. Those are the kinds of grades you cannot afford to throw away. You may find yourself in the uncomfortable position of prioritizing work from one class over work from another. Sometimes you just can't spend as much time on everything as you would like. Figure out what's worth the most and plan accordingly. You don't want to spend all your time freaking out over an assignment worth 5 percent for one class, only to discover an essay worth 40 percent of another class has come due and you haven't started.

Your grades will be determined in a variety of ways intended to serve different purposes. Sometimes your creativity and talents will really be challenged, and sometimes the only thing at issue will be your ability to jump through hoops in the proper order. It can be hard to perform well at something if you feel a particular exercise is unfair, unreasonable, or just plain silly. But if you can't take the work seriously as a real measure of your abilities and what you've learned, then take it seriously as a game. Do well at it because you've got years to spend in university anyway. You might as well get good grades instead of poor ones.

Busy Work

Often classes will include some component, perhaps 10 percent, reserved for short take-home assignments, pop quizzes based on memorization, or similarly simple work. This is the kind of work where if you do your reading, pay reasonable attention, and just hand things in on time, you're probably going to get at least eight out of ten. These are easy grades, so get them while you can. Some people find this kind of work frustrating or mechanical, but that's no excuse to throw away easy grades.

Honest professors will admit they frequently assign work like this just to ensure students do the readings and keep up with the class. I don't blame them, because they sure don't enjoy giving lectures to classrooms full of students who haven't done their readings, and who stare blankly back at them with nothing to say. This need for busy work gets back to a clash of priorities. A student who is eager to learn doesn't need this artificial incentive, and probably feels it's a waste of time. A student motivated by careerism will do the work gladly, and scoop up the easy grades, but may be annoyed if there are no practical applications to the exercise. Most everyone else is just glad to get ready signs of progress and credit for going through the appropriate motions.

It's one thing to play the game and take easy grades where you find them, but don't confuse pop quizzes and one-word answers with real evaluation. It's a very poor method of grading and it won't tell you anything about your progress as a student, or your skills in a subject area. It will reward you for keeping up with the assigned work, and this might come along with other benefits, but of itself it proves nothing.

Participation

Participation grades have got to be the most subjective thing going, and everyone knows it. The very idea of participation grades is interesting though, because it implies all kinds of priorities in education. In pure academia, there's a certain assumption that learning is a shared experience. Engaged students can motivate and encourage other students, and that's a nice ideal to aim for. In a way it's also good citizenship, and contributes to a lot of those important life lessons we've been talking about. Career-minded students tend to dislike participation grades because these grades feel arbitrary (and they are), and because too many like-minded students in a class will lead to a competition to talk the most every day. Sometimes it's interesting to hear what other students in the class think about the material, but it's hard to care what that guy who always talks has to say, especially when you know he's mainly saying it for credit. For the rest — the student looking for certification and the really lost ones — participation is frequently a chore (or even a real terror), and more motivated voices tend to drown them out.

In addition to the obvious goal of encouraging

participation in class, instructors use the flexibility of these grades to impose some justice on what is otherwise a frequently unjust system. Is there a student who's trying really hard but just not seeing results? Someone sitting there with a 68% or 69%? Well, a bit of tweaking on that participation grade can push her over the edge to a 70%. Conversely, that guy who never shows up to class but hands in really good assignments isn't going to get much slack. Participation grades are a levelling mechanism. Or at least they are for lectures. And when it comes to lectures, especially large ones, there are ways to get that grade that don't involve putting your hand up in class. You can hang around after class and ask the professor a few questions, or even just listen in on what other students are asking. You can go to the professor's office hours and do the same thing. You can even e-mail in a question or two every once in a while. More and more, you are likely to see some option for participation through on-line discussion and interaction. At the end of the year, the measure of a good participation grade, especially in a larger class, might be as simple as whether or not the professor actually knows who you are.

If there's a participation grade for tutorials, that's a different story. In that case there's no substitute for showing up to the tutorial, saying something useful, and otherwise just staying awake. Compared with writing an original essay, that's not so bad, right? It isn't easy for some students to talk in class, but the nice thing about tutorials is the smaller setting, and really it shouldn't be that hard to talk in front of a small group at least once in a while. This definitely falls within the range of general life skills you might as well learn sooner rather than later, because after school, wherever you go, the ability to express an opinion will prove valuable. For anyone other than the terminally shy, these are very easy grades — you can score nearly perfect just by showing up and talking — so scoop them up!

Competition and Weeding Out

From a purely utilitarian perspective, grades serve to identify the "good" students who should go further with their education (if they wish) from the ones who probably shouldn't. It's harsh to say, but probably a hundred or more students show up in first year, with the intention to become doctors, for every one that will have even a realistic shot at medical school by the end. In a case like this, the grading process serves to identify the students who belong in med school.

It's harsh, but honest. Our society only needs so many doctors; med schools have only so many places, and so they go to the most able students.

The folks running science programs, and other areas that focus on cold hard facts, tend to be pretty upfront that their grading system is designed to pressure students in a way that will sort quickly between those who can hack it and those who can't. Students who can't manage the workload may not fail necessarily, but they'll get the kind of grades that clearly indicate they aren't going further in that particular area. Some delude themselves anyway — through two, three, or even four years of mediocre grades — but at least they had evidence in hand that it just wasn't happening for them.

From the perspective of anyone who is really vocationally driven, this is what grading is all about. It can get pretty discouraging if the grades aren't saying what you wish they would say, but even negative feedback can be useful if it pushes you in the right direction sooner rather than later. This function of grading doesn't really get in the way of those students more motivated by citizenship, credentialism, or even just putting in time — because it's more about picking the really good students out from the pack. Limiting the number who do really well doesn't dictate that anyone else has to fail. When it feels as though the system is conspiring against you, it's useful to remember this. Sure, you can't all "win" in the sense that you all get grades that will allow you to go to med school, law school, or complete Ph.D.'s. But no one has to "lose" to the extent of flunking out

> Even negative feedback can be useful if it pushes you in the right direction sooner rather than later.

or failing courses.

Academically minded students are again at odds with this function, intended to serve primarily vocational goals. The students who are really into learning have future goals too, usually associated with graduate school, but they often aren't served well by the kind of take-no-prisoners sorting that happens in a first-year chemistry course. This is mostly a problem in science programs, rather than the arts, as they tend to focus early on memorization and a strict right/wrong grading structure. Sometimes students who are potentially very good just don't show up well when tested in this way. Graduate work won't emphasize the same skills anyway, and will focus instead on creativity, insight, and original thinking. So the system can send the wrong message if it spits out results too early that suggest these students aren't the ones who should progress.

The entire idea of identifying the "best" students from the pack can be tough on those who don't make the cut. In high school, everyone hears about how they'll be competing with better students in university, and against a higher standard, but somehow almost everyone is sure they will be the ones to come out on top of that stiffer competition. Of course it can't work out that way for everyone. Education is a gradually narrowing competition at a very specific kind of achievement. If you find your talents in this kind of competition top out as an undergraduate, that's hardly the worst fate imaginable. There are plenty of other reasons, and probably better ones, to feel good about yourself in this world.

The best you can do with the competitive aspect of

grading is just accept that it's going on, and take the information for what it's worth. Sometimes the methods of grading genuinely don't reflect the goal. If your goal is to get into teachers' college but you aren't very good at memorizing your textbooks, maybe that's not the worst thing. In later years, testing will move away from that kind of memorization, and you'll be better off. If you're trying to get into medical school, however, you're going to face that kind of expectation for a long time because it's simply part of the field. If you aren't good at it now, that should tell you something. So consider what your grades are actually telling you in relation to what you want. And if you still aren't sure, that's what academic advising and career counselling are for. Keep in mind that there are more and less effective ways to study for a test that requires a lot of memorization, and even more and less effective ways to write a multiple-choice exam. Look for help with those skills, if you find you aren't good at them.

Significant Feedback

One of the most glaring ways the distance between various priorities at university becomes apparent is when you consider the kind of feedback you receive on your work. If you write a multiple-choice exam, there might not be room for feedback beyond simply pointing out the right answers where you've failed to provide them, but if you do almost any work more substantial than this, you have a right to expect some advice for improvement. If you write an essay, you want more than just a grade; you also want some ideas about how you can do better next time. If you prepare a lab report and get less than perfect, you'd hope to know what you did wrong so you can get it right next time. That's just common sense, right? But think about all the times you've received nothing back but a letter or a numerical grade. No comments, no substantial feedback, no sense of where you went wrong, or even where you went right. Isn't there something a little off about that?

This sort of thing upsets academically minded students who want to know how they are really doing beyond the grades. It also tends to upset career-focused students, at least any time they aren't hauling in top grades, because they want to know where they lost marks. Other students are often just relieved to know they are still getting by and passing everything acceptably. But that's all you'll ever get out of a bare letter grade. It's enough to tell you that everything is "fine" if that's all you care about. But that's a pretty narrow idea of education, and an unfortunate result of mass production. Class size and pressure on instructors and teaching assistants cut into their ability to give meaningful and personal feedback. So students get a sense of how they are doing in a course, but not how they can improve. At least half the purpose of grading gets lost as a result.

This whole book is intended to help you arrive at some reason to care about university in order to get more out of it, and to provide you with some strategies to support that. I don't expect you to suddenly turn into an A student if you weren't one already. I certainly don't expect that to happen if your goals aren't focused on graduate or professional programs, but I do hope you end up interested enough to want to improve yourself. If you want to learn in university, and get better at the things you are doing and studying, then it should piss you off any time you get back some piece of work and don't have any idea where your grade came

Whether your grade is good, bad, or average, you deserve to know why it's that grade and not some other grade.

from. Whether your grade is good, bad, or average, you deserve to know why it's that grade and not some other grade. That way you might be able to do better next time. This isn't just about being a grades hound now; it's about wanting a quality education. Grading that evaluates what you know without giving you any indication of how to improve in the future is piss-poor education, and you deserve better.

If you don't understand where your grade came from, you should hit your professor's office hours and find out. Or go to your teaching assistant first, if you have one, and if that's what you are expected to do. The point is you should find out. And if you ever try to appeal your grade and argue for a higher one, it's best to approach the topic from the same perspective. Any worthwhile instructor will respect your intention if you say, "Look, I don't necessarily want a higher grade, but I don't understand this one and I think I deserve to." Then if you find the explanation isn't sufficient, you might come out with a better grade. Don't hold your breath about getting extra marks out of the conversation, because that's always a long shot, but either way you've got at least something from the experience because you stand to do better next time — which is rather the point, after all, of both education and evaluation. Improving your performance in the future is worth far more than a few extra marks on one assignment right away.

Too Cool for School

We all know this stuff from high school, right? A lot of kids simply don't want to be there and that comes out in a variety of ways. Trips to the bathroom are like get-out-of-jail-free cards. People sit at the back of the room like it's some kind of privilege to get as far away from the education as possible. Teacher absenteeism is cause for celebration, and the best kind of field trip is the kind that involves no real learning. You'd think all of this would end at the gates of "higher" learning, but it doesn't, somehow. It continues, if for no other reason, through force of habit.

Treating university education as though it's some kind of punishment makes no sense at all, on the surface. You pay to be there. You have a choice. Like I keep saying, thousands of dollars of your money, and years of your lifetime. No one would spend thousands of dollars on a car, then sit in it resentfully, refusing to drive it anywhere because it isn't good enough. And yet that's exactly what happens at every university every day. There are always at least some students, perhaps not many but some, who approach the whole thing resentfully. So what gives?

> No one would spend thousands of dollars on a car, then sit in it resentfully, refusing to drive it anywhere because it isn't good enough.

The most obvious answer is that some students don't have a choice, or at least don't have any choice they acknowledge. Life is full of choices we don't acknowledge, so let's try to be fair to those students who think they must be in university. As a kid, at twelve years old, you don't really have to be in school. You have the choice to run away from home. Of course that really isn't a choice at all, and most of us agree with this, but we have to admit it's at least possible. Flash forward six or seven years, and some kids, though technically now young adults, are still convinced they have no choice. Okay, they could move out of their parents' homes and find jobs, but for some this is literally as unthinkable as running away from home at age twelve. Right, wrong, or otherwise, these are people who have convinced themselves they have to be in university, or rather they have been convinced of this by family, friends, counsellors, and society in general. And make no mistake about it, it's a disservice to everyone involved, especially those poor kids suffering through it.

Sometimes it's obvious when someone just hates school or is trying desperately to ignore it. When you're asleep with your head on the desk, there isn't much subtlety to that. On an early Monday morning after a crazy weekend, you might be excused once in a while, but when you start to regard your lectures as afternoon nap time, there's clearly something wrong. Sometimes it's less obvious. How about those two friends who sit in the back of the room and whisper to each other the whole lecture? How about that guy in front of you who's got his laptop open but is playing solitaire? Or the couple who sit giggling and passing love notes? It's easy to pass over this kind of behaviour with a nod and a shrug, lending it a casual kind of legitimacy. That's just the way it is sometimes, right? Well, no, frankly it still makes no sense. You wouldn't pay to see a movie and act like that. Why pay for school, which costs a lot more, and then ignore it?

Various Dos and Don'ts

You can't police the students around you, so don't even try. At the same time, there's no reason you need to buy into habits that presuppose education is to be avoided whenever possible. See that behaviour for what it is and stay away from it. Maybe it makes sense in high school, to a point, but it's only going to cost you in university.

Don't sit in the back of the classroom. It's noisy back there, filled primarily with students who feel some obligation to show up but who would really rather not be there. Exceptions will occur, but I'm sure there's a steady drop in average grade the farther back you get. If you don't want to sit in the front, then compromise and at least sit in the middle. But you could do a lot worse than sitting right up front.

In high school, many students frown on that kind of initiative, and act as though it's somehow pretentious. If you're still afraid to appear too interested in university, you might want to get over that as soon as possible. The real world does not reward people who think that trying hard or showing interest is stupid.

> If you're still afraid to appear too interested in university, you might want to get over that as soon as possible.

Don't bring a friend or significant other to class. Definitely don't plan your schedule around a friend or significant other. There can be definite benefits to studying with a friend, especially if you work well in groups, but that doesn't mean you have to sit next to each other every lecture. If you are really disciplined and lay the ground rules carefully, you might find you can sit next to a friend, and if that works for you, fine. But if you find yourself chatting in class, you'd be better off sitting alone. If you look around, you'll see a lot of students sit by themselves every day. That isn't because they're anti-social or have no friends; it's because they're serious. Consider adopting a similar policy. It's a lot harder to be distracted when you remove yourself from distractions.

Don't be afraid to ask questions because other students might judge you. If you aren't comfortable speaking in front of the class or don't have any questions, it isn't the end of the world, but if you do have questions, you should absolutely ask them. The idea that people will mock you for raising your hand in class is something to get over fast. Do it all the time, or consistently say stupid things, and people might be unimpressed, but the simple act of asking a question is no longer cause for comment. Absolutely go to your professor's office hours if you want to discuss something further, e-mail questions, or participate in any discussion groups and options that may be available.

> Don't be afraid to ask questions because other students might judge you.

Don't feel grateful for opportunities to avoid education; feel cheated. Some students would be thrilled to have a professor take the majority of a term off, cancel every other lecture, and then test everyone on something meaningless in order to arrive at a set of grades. Some students would cheer. *Easiest class ever!* Well, you're paying for an education. Or someone else is paying for you, and I've got to assume their pockets aren't bottomless — eventually you'll run out of chances to get value from your opportunities. If you're just as glad to not get what you are paying for, that's an issue with your priorities you'll have to straighten out. Otherwise, there are ways to address the problem of a runaway professor. Talk to your students' union or council for a start, or approach the department chair directly. Not every problem gets fixed the way you'd like, but at least don't treat it as an occasion to celebrate.

If all this sounds like an awful lot of work, or it seems as though I'm pushing the whole education thing too hard and you wonder where all the parties and beer have gone, well, they're still there. Sure you can go out and party, though you should probably save it for the weekend if you can. Just remember that all these other symptoms of "too cool for school" tend to disappear in later years. Makes you wonder where all the sleepy and resentful students have gone. Two possible answers. Either they've wised up, or they've flunked out. Either way, you are best off coming to terms with it sooner rather than later.

Finally, and this is the last bit of advice I can give to anyone falling into these traps, try to draw a clear dividing line between your school and your social life. This can be hard sometimes, especially if you live on or near campus, but it needs to be done. You can't get work done when you're trying to socialize, and you can't really socialize and have much fun when you know you should be studying, listening to a lecture, or finishing an assignment. Even your social life will go more smoothly if you clearly separate your time for school and your time for fun.

Try to draw a clear dividing line between your school and your social life.

Understanding the Anger

Maybe you're the kind of person who doesn't need

any of the advice I just gave. Maybe for you, it's even obvious. Many people have great experiences at university, despite some awareness of the problems. To them, it can be distracting and even insulting to be around someone who just can't shut up about how much everything sucks. Maybe you've met a couple of these people. If you get really interested in the system, it's hard not to run into them. There's usually at least someone on a public crusade to expose how awful everything is, just as there's probably some kind of glee squad (official or otherwise) on a permanent mission to tell everyone how great everything is. If the debate is playing out in campus media and through student politics, you can choose to ignore it, with a little willpower. But maybe your own friends are pushing one perspective or another and you can't avoid the discussion, no matter how much you wish to. If you think it's just your school, you're wrong. This happens at the little community colleges and at the Ivy League schools too. But wherever you are it's definitely a real downer, when you're having a pretty decent time, to have someone trying to convince you you're wrong. You can't both be right, can you?

> You can have a positive and rewarding experience at university while some other poor sucker has an awful time, even though you're in exactly the same place.

Well, yes, actually you can both be right. You can have a positive and rewarding experience at university while some other poor sucker has an awful time, even though you're in exactly the same place. If you fall into the trap of thinking that university is the same experience for everyone, it may feel very important to convince the people around you they're having the same experience as you. Of course they aren't. But that's why it feels so personal when that guy tries to tell you it sucks, and that's also why he's so frustrated when you don't agree. The only thing worse than feeling cheated is feeling cheated in a crowd of people who seem to say you haven't been cheated. When you put yourself in that guy's shoes, even if you don't share his opinion, it's pretty clear why he's so upset.

I don't have any magic words for the students who feel swindled. In this case, the problem with university is no different than the general problems with our society and western materialism. We've all been raised to expect a certain degree of material and professional success, and the pressures of these expectations can be crushing, especially for young people who don't have a clue what they want to do with their lives. University is sold as the next step, and often as the answer to every question that hasn't made sense before, and when that turns out to be false, it's pretty disappointing. So some people take out their frustrations on the institution and blame it for everything, which doesn't help at all. But it might be understandable, at least. People who don't know what they want out of university shouldn't be there, but aside from this advice I can't make it suck any less if you feel like you *must* be there. All I can do is point out that you have a choice.

You don't need the opinions of the people around you to validate your experiences at university. Differing opinions about university merely reflect different sorts of experiences, of which there are many. Taken from that perspective, the people who can't shut up about how much university sucks are only expressing the problems they've encountered. That's a voice that needs to be heard. Don't resent the messengers; pay attention to the message. University is quite clearly failing at least some people, and it's important to see that, even if it isn't failing you.

Competing Agendas and Politicization

Entirely aside from competing ideas of what university should be doing for students, there are competing ideas of what university should be doing in society. Sometimes you'll hear about this as a question of "politicizing" university, but that's an inexact statement, leveraged by people who simply want to register their disapproval. Should university be a primary mechanism of capitalism, focused entirely on turning out a skilled workforce? The promotion of capitalism does imply an agenda. Should university serve as a venue to question our political status quo, hosting conferences that advocate widespread social reform? Obviously that's an agenda also. University is inevitably political in various ways, so pointing that out isn't news.

Universities occupy prominent positions in society, and for good or for ill, they are often at the centre of political controversy. This shouldn't be surprising. It's long been recognized that control of the children today translates into control of the political agenda tomorrow. As the proportion of young people attending post-secondary institutions increases, for those with any vested interest, it only becomes more and more vital to steer the politics of those institutions as much as possible. And so we come back around to the basic question of what goes on in a school. Or to put it another way, what should education concern itself with?

What Is

Probably the least controversial function of university is to simply teach accepted facts and theories. Of course even that can generate some controversy, because what's "accepted" is always up for grabs, and folks will still dispute things like the theory of evolution, but generally speaking so long as universities stay focused on facts, figures, and hard information, they are on safe ground. To most sensibilities, it's pretty clear that education is going well when young minds get filled with old knowledge.

This agenda runs into problems, especially at research-based universities, because it might be all well and good for undergraduate education to simply repeat and reinforce accepted wisdom, but the mission of the academy as a whole reaches further. Professors conduct research, which frequently challenges accepted wisdom or attempts to extend what is known, and the best and most effective forms of education integrate this kind of inquiry. The goal is to produce lifelong learners who are not only trained in established knowledge, but also equipped to learn new things on their own. So despite the occasional efforts of the most practically minded — sometimes including parents, industry, governments, etc. — undergraduate education inevitably steps beyond the confines of simply teaching what is already known and begins to explore new ideas.

What Might Be

This is the kind of question that tends to get academics in trouble. Every once in a while, one of them asks a "what if" sort of question that pisses everyone off and hits the headlines. Most of the time the exploration of new ideas isn't news at all. If a chemist sits down to try to figure out a new way to combine molecules, it isn't a revolutionary act. The results might be significant, but the mere act of exploring the question is not. In fact, university professors are always exploring these sorts of ideas, in their own fields and in their own ways, so probably 99.9 percent of the time what they do isn't even vaguely controversial. A unique perspective on Joseph Conrad might win an English professor recognition in her field, but no one else is likely to even notice.

And then some geneticist comes along and decides he wants to see if intelligence can be correlated along racial lines. Or an economist decides to question the entire set of assumptions that underlie the policies of the World Bank. Or an environmental scientist suggests that accepted wisdom about recycling might be flawed, that the whole endeavour could be ultimately futile. And all hell breaks loose. It isn't the conclusions that are offensive; it's even asking the question that upsets people. And that's fascinating. Most lifelong academics would argue there are very few offensive questions, as long as they are approached objectively, but apparently the rest of the world doesn't agree.

This is where a clash of priorities starts to really show up. There aren't many issues that can get almost all academics to agree on a point of principle,

but intellectual freedom, and the ability to ask any question in order to pursue new knowledge (even the kind that might upset people), is one of those issues. Even controversial ideas should have room for exploration, though perhaps with a sensible dose of tact. This makes perfect sense if you see university as a place that generates new knowledge. Otherwise, perhaps not. But when push comes to shove, most governments and industries support this function of university. Though they do seem far more interested in knowledge generation when it produces new chemical compounds than when it produces new theories about Joseph Conrad.

What Should Be

There is another vision of university that rarely appears in mission statements or constitutions, and doesn't tend to get discussed in governance meetings, but is very real nonetheless. It's the vision of university that sees angry students marching in hordes to go protest something, or raising money to support some cause or other. It's a vision of university that might conjure, for many, some association with Berkeley and Vietnam War protests.[1] Academics and administrators might not acknowledge this idea of what university is and does, but to many students, and often to political activists, university isn't only about facts as they are understood, and things as they might be discovered, but also about what should be. They see the university setting as a vehicle for social change. And popular culture, if nothing else, seems to support this idea.

From the perspective of a student most interested in improving the experience of university, the set of

motivations I've broadly called good citizenry, this function of university tends to make a lot of sense. Young people are exposed to new ideas, situations, and questions. They naturally want to go out and test them. So university becomes a rallying ground for cutting edge social issues, and sometimes those issues even creep into the structure of the institution itself. Academia, for example, tends to be on the forefront of asking questions about equity practices. Student organizations often go even further, initiating all kinds of different programs aimed at correcting the general ills of society. For some, this initiative represents everything that makes the university experience special. For others, it's frustrating to find the institution so far out of step with the rest of the world.

Students start to express their values very directly, and even aggressively in their activities on campus, and some can get very offended by people who don't agree with them. I don't have any easy answers about how to cope with this. Politically active students decry the "apathy" of people who just want to learn, and sometimes even bring their activism into the classroom. Academically minded students can't deal with the idea that freedom of inquiry should be subject to a social agenda. Students focused on getting their qualifications and getting out frequently do their best to just stay out of the way. It's easy to feel as though the students around you are screwing up your experience again. Recognizing this problem of differing priorities can help you relate to what's up with the students you share space with. If you ever find yourself in a debate where there's no room for compromise on either side, maybe you can shift it toward a more general dialogue on the role university can or should play in the promotion of social change. You might find you have more common ideological ground than you realize, but simply don't agree on the time and place for such things.

Private or Public, Consumer or User?

Sometimes it's hard for students to establish their proper relationship to university, especially in an environment that sends such mixed messages about the status of the institution in society. If universities are private, then they are subject to market forces, and students (and their parents) should rightly consider themselves customers. If universities are public, then students (and their parents) are still paying a lot of money for the privilege of attending, but it seems more like a big-ticket user fee than a free-market purchase.

The United States draws a clear distinction among its colleges (universities) by recognizing both "private" colleges and "public" ones. The major bit of criteria that distinguishes private from public is that public institutions are supported extensively by the government, while private ones are not. This creates a partial two-tier system because tuition balloons in private colleges, creating an exclusive quality, but some public colleges are still very good, and not all private ones are first-rate, so the distinction isn't absolute. Likewise, the distinction between private and public isn't as sharp as it might appear at first glance. Private institutions still perform a service for the public, and receive various incentives such as tax breaks to do so, and public institutions may still enjoy substantial private endowments.

In Canada, we don't have private universities in the same sense as they exist in the States. All of our universities are supported by the government, which is to say that the government kicks in a certain amount of money to support the education of each domestic student enrolled. Nevertheless, our public universities often have very personal identities and traditions. They can't be considered public in the same sense that a park, a swimming pool, or a library is public. Lots of private money is running around these places, and lots of agendas come along with that money. One goal of every university, whether big or small, is to build up its endowment. Endowed money helps the university to finance its own priorities rather than submit to the agenda of government. So within any university, notions of public and private exist in an uneasy balance, and the issue is as real in Canada as it is in the United States.

Now, I'm sure you're wondering how that matters to the average student, but you encounter expressions of this issue all the time — you simply may not recognize it. Often students try to approach university as customers. This feels wrong to a lot of people, but there's some validity to it. The more universities push their product in a competitive marketplace, the more they are just begging to be regarded as service providers, and the more they invite students to regard themselves as customers. But if students are customers and they are buying an awfully expensive product, then that old consumer adage starts to nag at us and seems to say, "The customer is always right." Well, if that's the case, then why should the customer ever fail?

Students as Consumers

There's a story about the big private American colleges that some academics like to tell as a way of attacking the notion that their quality of education is invariably better. Students (or more likely their parents) pay tens of thousands of dollars per year in tuition. Many of them come from families with so much money, it makes career professors look working class. And that can erode the position of respect a little bit. So when the grades come back and unhappy students show up at the professor's office, it's a little different than what you might be used to.

They aren't just disappointed and trying to beg an extra mark or two. Those students show up with all the fury of outraged consumers, and say things like, "I'm not paying $30,000 a year to get a B minus!" And they mean it. And the saddest part is the institution has to bow, at least a little bit, to these pressures. Grade inflation becomes a problem.

Fortunately we don't have that kind of problem in Canada just yet, but the tension still exists as an undercurrent. Prior to university, in high school and earlier, the relationship is pretty obvious. Students are basically wards of the government while they are in public school. But come university (or college), things change. Now you're paying money to be there. Shouldn't you have the right to demand something? It feels wrong somehow that you are still interacting with the system as though it owns you, as though you should feel grateful if you can just keep your head above water. And that is wrong. But it is also wrong to assume you are entitled to good grades just because you paid to be there. Where's the balance?

Certification students probably have the most natural grasp of the balance as it currently exists. If you think of university as similar to any other licensing process, such as the place where you go to get your driver's license, most of the rest comes fairly clear. Of course you aren't entitled to pass your driver's test just because you pay the evaluation fee. You still need to meet all the appropriate standards, and if you don't, you fail, even though you are "the customer." Same thing at university. But university doesn't just function as a

> If you think of university as similar to any other licencing process, such as the place where you go to get your driver's license, most of the rest comes fairly clear.

licensing office, it's also the driving school. So when you fail your test, does that mean you just didn't meet the standard, or does it suggest, perhaps, that you weren't adequately prepared to pass? And if so, doesn't that suggest a justifiable complaint?

This is where an academic perspective comes in handy. You are paying for an education, and if it isn't adequately delivered, then of course you have a right to complain. Even if you'd rather not learn today, you've got to realize that it'll only cost you tomorrow. If anything happens to go wrong, you won't be compensated with free grades, despite the odd notion some students develop that the university "owes" them. The university owes you every reasonable opportunity to succeed, but if the education and evaluation processes fail, the university does not owe you the benefit of the doubt that you know what you're doing. You won't get a default A just because your class got all messed up, any more than you'll get your driver's license by default just because your test got all messed up. At most you'll get a do over.

If your professor is scattered, ill prepared, neglectful, or just plain absent, then of course you have a justifiable complaint and you should express it. Don't wait all year then expect free grades. I promise it won't work. Complain early, complain loudly, complain *respectfully*, and make your case. University seems so important (and it is) that students are sometimes amazed it's even possible for a course to go off the rails, but when there are hundreds of courses offered every year, odds dictate at least something crazy will happen. Some professor is going to get hit by a bus. Or the one classroom with a vital technical resource will be off-line. Or the university actually went and hired someone who is blatantly incompetent. The best hiring process in the world will fail sometimes, and it's sad, but it does happen. *Then* you get to act like an outraged consumer.

Sometimes a course doesn't go entirely wrong but some administrative elements, perhaps including methods of evaluation, get thrown completely out of whack. Vocational students, with a sharp eye on the grades they need to get into whatever place they are aiming for, are often very aware of this issue. You'll hear them complain quickly and loudly whenever something isn't fair. Now, "fair" is a very subjective idea, and frequently students are far too quick to complain about things they don't feel are fair, but it's also true that sometimes things get genuinely messed up. Sometimes as a result, the outcomes aren't fair. Truly unfortunate things can happen, such as a crucial error on the exam, or maybe the use of a new teaching assistant who doesn't have a clue how to grade. It's rare but it happens. Just as it's appropriate to get vocal when you aren't receiving the education you pay for, it's also fair to get vocal when the methods of evaluation fail. You're also paying for a level system of assessment and accreditation. Just be extra careful you approach this properly, because as I've already said, students complain far too often about how things are "unfair" when they simply don't like the outcome. You'll have to make your case properly to establish that your situation is different.

> If you ever need to complain about the conduct of a course, or of a professor, be sure you concentrate on what's gone wrong with the education and/or the system of evaluation.

If you ever need to complain about the conduct of a course, or of a professor, be sure you concentrate on what's gone wrong with the education and/or the system of evaluation. Don't focus on outcomes — "I deserved a higher grade!" — but concentrate instead on process. What went wrong? How did it disrupt the normal learning process? And if, on that basis, you think you have a legitimate gripe, then go right ahead and pursue it. Go to the department head if you feel confident enough to get right into it; go to academic advising if you want to talk with a university employee who knows the system; try your student representatives if you want a more direct advocate. When something happens that isn't supposed to happen, it can be tough, at times, to figure out where to go. Not everyone will be adequately prepared to help you. But if you keep at it, you will get help. Bring your classmates on-board with your concerns, if it is an issue affecting everyone, because there's strength in numbers.

If you want to contact the chair of a department or another senior administrator, with an issue of this nature or a similar concern, you might really be shocked at how seriously they'll take a well-presented complaint. Very few students take the initiative to do this sort of thing, so it always gets noticed when it happens. Provided you are serious and mature in your approach, it will almost certainly reflect well on you, rather than badly, that you've taken some initiative to correct a perceived problem. Even if you don't get the outcome you would like, it won't damage your reputation in the department, and may actually distinguish you. It's never fun when you are forced to deal with something that's gone wrong, but even a bad situation can be an opportunity to show you can handle it well.

Faculty as Service Providers

Students aren't the only ones feeling the pressure of this looming tension between public and private, and between student consumers and student users. Professors and lifelong academics inevitably confront the same issues as well. Remember that most career academics fall within that grouping of people who believe in education for its own sake, and many of them are involved with instruction at the undergraduate level as a means to support their research. They view this undercurrent between students and faculty, suggestive of a customer-service provider relationship, to be very troubling. Not only does this undercut their status in the lecture hall (very important to most professors), but it brings into question their ideals as lifelong students. Add to this the additional pressures of growing class sizes, limited resources and support, and all the other potential problems and tensions at work in university today, and it isn't surprising that some professors are getting discouraged. These problems are just as real for them as they are for you.

It's almost always a bad idea to approach your instructors as service providers. It's definitely a bad idea if you're going to be disrespectful about it. In a few limited cases, especially in vocational programs that employ a lot of lecturers drawn from industry, this perspective might be more acceptable and more valid. A management program, for example, might support this view as long as respect is maintained. But in all classic academic areas, it's a very bad idea to even hint at this sort of relationship. However you happen to feel about it privately, even if you feel this is an appropriate parallel, it won't get you very far, so you might as well fake it. The good news, at least, is that many professors are just as concerned about the quality of education as you are. If you ever want to discuss the subject and express your concerns, you'll probably find a sympathetic ear, and you may have a very interesting discussion on the topic. The bad news is that your professor might agree with you entirely, but still be powerless to address your complaints. You may learn that much of what goes on in the classroom, even if it seems your professor is behind it, is the result of decisions and conditions over which she has very little control.

Almost all professors and instructors, even the ones primarily interested in their own research, and even those disillusioned by current trends in higher education, love an engaged and concerned student. One of the most frequent concerns expressed by faculty, on the subject of expanding class size, is that they can't get to know individual students. But there are always a few that stand out anyway. I talk a lot about the need to empathize with the students around you, and to stop seeing them as part of the problem, even if you don't agree with their priorities. Well, the next step in that process is to empathize, if you can, with your professors and instructors, and to stop seeing them as part of the problem. Aside from a few bad apples, most instructors are just good people trying to operate in less than ideal circumstances. If you can have a mature conversation on the subject, you'll not only benefit by distinguishing yourself from the masses, you might even help your professor to feel a little better as well, simply because he now knows one more student who is genuinely engaged.

Eroding Value and Graduating "Everyone"

The university experience can be awfully frustrating for those who are looking at their degree as a ticket to material success or social status. Tradition has taught us to regard university education as a rather exclusive privilege, and frequently family and popular culture continue to support this view. The reality on the ground is now quite different. As greater and greater numbers of young people continue through to college and university, and as more and more of them acquire degrees and diplomas, any hope that the degree alone will be enough to guarantee "success" is quickly lost. You've only got to show up at one lecture with a class size in the hundreds to realize that the exclusive quality disappeared some time ago. And depending on your

STILL THINKS A UNIVERSITY EDUCATION IS EXCLUSIVE.

perspective, this can be frustrating in the extreme. Many students find it a major blow to their motivation, and — since motivation is a major key to success — that's a serious problem.

From the perspective of students simply interested in learning, it isn't a huge problem that lots of other people are also learning. For students interested in life lessons and good citizenry, the size and scope of the community is certainly no deterrent and might even be exciting. Of course individual tastes vary, and some would prefer a more intimate environment, but there's nothing that hinders a student learning those sorts of life lessons by being around other students doing the same. Greater resources are devoted to senior students, and in upper-year courses the class size tends to narrow down as subjects become more specialized. But the basic condition hasn't gone away. There are *many* more students in university today than there once were.

It's vocational students, and especially certification students, that really feel the pinch when so many others receive the same qualifications. Many vocationally minded students want or need to continue further and gain additional qualifications, and it's disheartening to hit the point where "success" is supposed to be assured only to find there's a whole new field of competition to beat in order to become an accountant, veterinarian, pharmacist, or whatever. For anyone with those goals firmly in mind, the prospect of hitting the job market with "only" an undergraduate degree, if the bid for professional or graduate school isn't successful, is distinctly scary — hardly less so than job-hunting directly out of high school. Certification students feel the crunch in their own way. Although they may plan on hitting the job market with their undergraduate degrees, the idea of so many other students doing the same is very discomforting.

As for holding-pen students, well, the whole mob scene at university probably allows them to coast a while longer, but that's hardly beneficial in the long run. They may find anonymity comforting at times, but they are certainly not well served by it.

Show Me the Money

From a purely market-driven perspective, the value of post-secondary education has taken a beating lately. The loss runs two ways. First, the price tag for the education is shooting way up. Second, the market value of that education in terms of earning potential is eroding. It isn't that post-secondary education is less important in today's employment market, perhaps quite the reverse, but as more and more students acquire the education, the earning power of the degree alone declines. If everyone has got one, even if everyone paid dearly for it, the distinction conveys no advantage. Of course we aren't at that extreme quite yet, but we are definitely moving in that direction.

For anyone concerned about the future earning power of a degree this is obviously a frustrating situation. There doesn't seem to be an alternative in sight, however. In the States, with their expensive private institutions, there appears to be at least the opportunity to purchase exclusivity, even if the price tag comes in the tens of thousands of dollars per year. Some advocate for a similar move in Canadian education, and deregulated tuition, where it exists, is a definite first move in this direction. But for now, at least, there isn't any guaranteed chance to buy your way into exclusivity. Unless, of course, you want to go study in the United States.

At the same time that the earning value of the degree is eroding, and the cost to acquire it climbing,

> At the same time that the earning value of the degree is eroding, and the cost to acquire it climbing, the government is caught in a situation where it has to justify ballooning student debt.

the government is caught in a situation where it has to justify ballooning student debt. And so we get the official line that it's still a good investment. According to most statistics, the investment in undergraduate education, even at today's tuition and in today's job market, eventually pays off.[2] And that's probably accurate. It doesn't stop students from feeling shafted, compared to previous generations of graduates, but considering the direction things seem to be heading, we're still all better off than students will be ten years from now, so it's hard to put that complaint into proper perspective until we see how bad things get. Of course the major problem with that "still profitable" argument is that it assumes the profit motive. What about those who have other motives?

Show Me the Education

The problem that follows from the cost of education is this overwhelming need to justify the cost. Statistics that show a university degree eventually pays off may placate vocational and certification students, to a point, but what about those students looking for pure learning, or else those seeking personal growth? Well, many would answer that regardless of motive those students are still going to graduate and get jobs one day, so the earning potential of the degree is still important and justifies the cost. Which is true. But it ignores what's happened to the education itself.

Universities have moved heavily into territory typically considered the domain of vocational schools, colleges, and similar institutions. More and more they are marketing programs that are directed at specific jobs. These programs are in demand, and so schools continue to innovate, providing more programs of this nature. But why this sudden demand? It would be absurd to treat this new drive for practical education as a separate and incidental trend. Students are driven more and more to seek practical education as a sort of safeguard. When it's costing you so damn much it had better be practical. Who wants an unmarketable degree with a $25,000 debt to show for it?

The reasoning behind making education more marketable appeals to certification and vocational students, but university is an integrated whole. So all students end up on the receiving end of this new focus on practical education — and the not-so-subtle message, if you read between the lines, that education for its own sake is rather frivolous. It's one thing when the various functions of university seem to get in each other's way. It's quite another thing when the government itself, through funding priorities and attached justifications, suggests the only right reason to get an education is to get a good income out of it.

It isn't that the government doesn't appreciate the value of pure learning. It isn't that the government doesn't appreciate the value of citizenship and life lessons. But when it comes time to justify the

skyrocketing costs of education and a lack of political
will to fund it better, no provincial government wants
to acknowledge the social good of higher education.
A focus on the social good implies a public obligation
to fund it. A focus on the personal gain implies every
reason in the world to load the cost on the individual.
And so we continue to move in this direction, and the
focus on investment and return becomes more and
more accepted in public discourse.

The Vicious Cycle and Fad Programs

Perhaps the worst expression of the increasing focus
on practical and marketable education is when
students are scared away from their natural interests,
and convinced to focus on areas presumed to be more
lucrative. We all know the story about the guy or girl
with a university degree waiting tables or pumping

gas to pay down the student debt, no real job in sight, and we sure don't want that to happen to us! So we rethink that English program, or (God forbid) philosophy, and maybe we take something like commerce instead. Ten years ago computer science would have been widely viewed as a guaranteed ticket to a good job. Of course that was before the whole industry collapsed. The IT industry has rebounded since, but any notion that it's invulnerable is hopefully done with.

I won't dictate a difference between good and bad motivations, but whatever you're going to do, you've got to care about it if you expect to succeed. You are far better off studying philosophy, and doing well at the subject, than you are grinding your way through some more "practical" degree and just scraping by. I think deep down most people know this. But we let those stories about waiting tables and pumping gas scare us, and we second-guess our better instincts. And maybe we try that other program anyway.

Here's the really ironic part. If you accept the idea that people will do well if they stick to things they care about, and there's always a job market for accomplished people, you've got to stop and ask yourself what happened to that guy pumping gas and that girl waiting tables. What hampered their success? How'd they end up back in service jobs even with degrees under their belts? Chances are they went and took something they didn't really care about. And for fear of ending up where they are now, you go and repeat exactly the same mistake.

It doesn't always break down that simply, I know, but we all keep hearing about this modern economy in which no job is safe, how we're all going to have several careers in our lifetimes. We nod, we take notes, and then we go looking for a sure thing anyway, even though we just heard it doesn't exist. The worst thing you can possibly do is jump on the bandwagon of the latest sure thing and take the program everyone else is taking — because there's obviously only a limited demand for people trained in any particular area. There might be a short-term boom in one sector or another, but when things settle down again only the people who are really good are going to hang on. That's what happened to the IT sector. In my opinion, we are heading in the same direction, with an over-saturation of commerce and management degrees right now. That's no reason to avoid commerce and management if you really care about those areas. Accomplished people will always be in demand, but it's a definite mistake to take something only because it's suddenly the thing to do, because everyone else is doing it.

The final expression of this formula that balances investment versus reward, and perhaps the most frustrating one of all, comes when you combine the trends of fad programs with the new reality of deregulated tuition. Universities will try to deregulate their fees when the market will bear the cost of what they want to charge. The market will forgive high tuition where there's a lot of demand and the promise of future income. That has "fad" written all over it. It's easy to imagine an expensive education must lead to a big payoff. And maybe sometimes that's true. But quite often it can be just the reverse as well. That, of all possible combinations of circumstances, is the biggest shame I can think of. To pay twice as much for an education in an area you don't really care about only to find the market flooded with other students who have the same qualifications, and then to compete with those who really care about the field, when you could have taken something you enjoy for half the price — and had all the advantages of natural talent and enthusiasm ... What has our system come to when students end up in that situation?

Study what you are good at and what you care about, no matter what you've heard about the gas station attendant or the waiter.

Bottom line: in a world with no guarantees, the best and only enduring advantage is to play to your strengths and not bank on trends. Study what you are good at and what you care about, no matter what you've heard about the gas station attendant or the waiter.

Why Does It Hang Together?

Perhaps the single biggest thing that doesn't make any sense about undergraduate university, at least on the surface, is why and how it could possibly hang together as a (mostly) coherent whole under the pressure of all these competing purposes. If university serves all these various needs — pure learning, vocational training, socialization, certification, and as a basic place to put young people — and if they are all so badly suited to one another, then why didn't the whole institution explode a long time ago?

For this final mystery, I can offer only a partial explanation. It seems to me that university is experiencing a crisis of identity and purpose while most of the players in the institution, and in government, are so committed to the system as it exists that re-envisoning the whole thing is too daunting to consider. That, and the fact that certain functions of university have become dependent on the whole even if the arrangement doesn't serve the needs of students.

Pure academia is perhaps most guilty. Universities keep churning out aspiring academics with Ph.D.'s and post-doctoral qualifications, and all these people need jobs. So it may not serve the interests of vocational, citizenry, or certification students to learn from these (otherwise unemployable) career academics, but that's how universities support their ongoing research, fund graduate programs, and keep the whole cycle continuing. Even universities without graduate programs or extensive research missions hire faculty based on academic credentials, rather than experience and teaching skills. No rule dictates it has to work this way. There are other educational systems, such as arts colleges and undergraduate teaching institutions, where career instructors rather than career academics teach students who are looking for more practical education. But if Canadian universities were to move very far in that direction, it would put a lot of professional academics and researchers out of work. Not surprisingly, universities, run by academics, aren't strong advocates of that kind of reform.

Vocational programs have a strange kind of double identity that motivates them to hang with the other functions of university, rather than come right out and say they are engaged in job training. There's

nothing at all wrong with job training, but whenever it's done on its own (say, at the college level), it seems to attract a stigma of being somehow lesser. So vocational training in university promises practical education that will lead students to jobs while maintaining the credibility that comes along with academia. Of course the distinction is only about optics, but it's a powerful distinction nonetheless. Students don't want diplomas in engineering, accounting, or forestry; they want university degrees. But they want the degree to be practical and marketable all the same. Faculty aren't entirely blameless here either. Even the most directly vocational programs employ professors who are eager to play up their academic cred, and to lay claim to the distinction of being a university professor in the field. And so the bad union continues.

Citizenship students are an interesting bunch. They could be happy in a lot of different settings. But there's still the general message that says university is the place to grow up and mature, and also that university is the place to flex your instincts to make the world a better place. University may be a good place to learn life lessons, but they are going to be specific life lessons. Of course the institution has certain values and ideals attached to it, many of them influenced by a vaguely leftist intellectual elite. Anyone with an interest in promoting those values will naturally want to present university as the place to learn and grow. In addition to the "default" university value set, there's a constant push from every side — every group and cause imaginable — to get their messages onto university campuses. They aren't doing this because citizenship-type students study there. The students who really care will find political groups and causes on their own time. The interest groups, rather, are trying to reach everyone else. If you can shape the young minds today, you can influence the direction of society tomorrow. So every cause interested in change or reform doesn't want to reach only those students who are likewise interested. They want, rather, to reach everyone at once, whether the people they reach are interested or not. As a result, university is a hotbed of politics and social agendas, regardless of the intentions of those students in attendance.

The certification function of university gets caught in the crossfire. If none of the other functions are differentiated, then certification from anywhere else just isn't going to cut it. Colleges offer general arts programs, but far too many people consider them a last option — for students who can't deal with university. As so often happens, the perception helps to create the reality, and real legitimacy is confined to university as a result. Colleges might offer strong and competitive vocational programs, in some cases, but their liberal arts programs can't compete. This is a shame for students who just want some certification to establish their general skills, because they are forced into the same system as those students looking to be doctors and lawyers, so must then take an all-or-nothing approach to education.

Holding-pen students are a symptom, not a cause, but they follow the pack. If not for the way the other functions hang together, it wouldn't even be possible to show up to university "just because." As it stands, we continue to present the illusion there is one thing going on, rather than several, and those students who don't yet have any concrete plans or ambitions follow along in the hope of finding that one thing. Their tuition helps to bankroll the system, however, so perhaps no one minds very much. Of course most of them get burned pretty badly before it's all over, but that's the part university administrators try not to talk about. It's fine to discuss students who "don't belong" in university — and to sigh, laugh, or wince as appropriate in context — but it's far more rare to question how or why they end up there anyway. If all those students stopped enrolling, it would cause huge problems, so no university administration is motivated to examine their role in this issue too closely.

The fact is that the system doesn't serve most

> If not for the way the other functions hang together, it wouldn't even be possible to show up to university "just because."

students very well, but the gatekeepers of the institution, and those most able to motivate change, are far too invested in the status quo. Academics need their jobs; vocational programs need their credibility; social-agenda types want to get their licks in at everyone at once; and anyone looking for a basic level of certification has to go where everyone else is heading. All of this contributes to what I call the universality of university, which I'll talk about next chapter.

---

1 UC Berkeley, and student activism centred there, played a significant role in early efforts to resist the Vietnam War and demonstrate public opposition to it. In addition to rallies and education initiatives, major activities included the burning of draft cards, and attempts to block railway trains carrying troops.

2 A couple of interesting studies on this topic appear in Kelly-Ann Rathje's and Herbert Emery's *Renovating the Ivory Tower: Canadian Universities and the Knowledge Economy.* In "Returns to University Education in Canada," Vaillancourt and Bourdeau-Primeau demonstrate that returns to both the individual and society remain strong, and therefore higher education remains a sound investment even at increased tuition. Rathje and Emery argue, on the basis of anticipated lifetime earnings, that tuition should rise dramatically (though at differentiated levels) in most areas of study. These positions, based on complex modelling, are typical of the perspective that economists tend to bring to the debate. But they do not adequately acknowledge the expanding client base of university, and have no formula to account for innate ability. To expect the same rates of return no matter how much of the population is educated, and regardless of who is educated, is deeply unrealistic. There's only so much room at the top of the earnings pyramid. And it's fine to show on paper that education pays off on average before retirement, but most teenagers aren't taking a forty-year view on such things. When the price tag alone starts scaring students away, or toward unnatural choices dictated by fear and economic pressures, there is more going on than just fair market pricing.

CHAPTER FIVE

THE BIG PICTURE

Beyond the Personal

I guess it's obvious by now that I'm pretty interested in what's going on at university. I showed up expecting to study English, political science, and maybe some philosophy, and I somehow ended up studying university itself. Well, education is funny that way: it tends to pull you off in unexpected directions. Which isn't a bad thing at all. Sometimes people find their callings that way.

If you just came to this book to look for direct and practical information, then I've given you most of what I can give you. The first four chapters are full of as much practical stuff as I can think to offer. But now I want to talk about the big-picture issues. I want to talk about some of the basic conditions that are causing problems in the first place. You might wonder how this is going to help you. Well, first, if you're anything like me, you take an interest in your surroundings. Call it a natural instinct to study whatever is at hand, if you identify as an academic. Call it simple pragmatism to know as much about your environment as possible, if you're more interested in your career options. From any perspective, it's just satisfying to be in a place that you understand, rather than one where you're constantly feeling lost.

The other thing I'd like to do, if I can, is to lay out the original conditions that contribute to the problems I've identified. Because I know I can't predict every single symptom of what's going on at university, or give you step-by-step instructions for every possible scenario, I'd like to challenge you, or at least give you the opportunity, to take these ideas further than I've taken them. Look for expressions of these problems in your own institution. Find ways that these issues play out, and maybe you'll be able to see solutions or opportunities you wouldn't have seen otherwise. And if you come up with anything really good, please let me know because I like learning new things too.

The Universality of University

University seems to have become the sole and exclusive path to "success" in the eyes of many people. This message is in our homes, in our family values, in our popular culture, everywhere. Near the end of high school, there's an almost tangible distance between those who intend to continue on to university, and those who do not or cannot. The educational system plays into this as well. It's all about what it takes to get into university. It's all about who is going, and who isn't. Depending on your background and environment, college may be a valid decision as well.

Of course everyone wants to be successful, and everyone wants their children to be successful, and our public education system is aimed at helping students to succeed. Behind all of this pressure is nothing more than good intentions. But pretending that there's one sure path to success in life, when we all want different things and have different priorities and value systems, is obviously flawed. One can argue that education is helpful regardless of your goals, but I hope by now I've also illustrated that there are different kinds of education suited to different sorts of goals. We obscure all of that under a single massive word when we say "university." I've spent this entire book trying to overcome the power of that one word. The word is backed by unthinkable amounts of cultural pressure. In most minds, two words, "university" and "success," are probably so closely linked, they are almost synonymous. Yet we don't all mean the same thing when we talk about success, and we mean so many different things when we talk about university. And so university becomes just the place that generates success.

All kinds of problems accumulate when people lose sight of what university is and does, and when people expect that success is simply a natural result of enrollment along with the regular payment of tuition. But the universality of university — the sheer weight of associations behind the institution — has other negative consequences. I think of these consequences as fetishisms. People get obsessed with the trappings, the incidental ceremonies of university. It's almost religious. Which shouldn't be surprising, as univer-

sities evolved from religious institutions in the first place. But the trappings and traditions, attractive as they may be, feed into the problem. It's so easy to get stuck thinking about symbols and time-honoured practices, to buy into the illusion of constancy, that we are easily deflected from examining the current reality. Among the biggest culprits that perpetuate the university's inflated significance are professors. After all, they only benefit. It's their status on the line.

Academic Superiority

There are many pressures at work in a modern university, and many agendas, but career academics still regard university as a place that's run by academics for academics. And most of the trappings and traditions support this notion. Although government and university-as-business administrators may shoulder in at the highest levels of administration, for students and for the public at large, the face of university remains the faculty. So if in popular view university has become the sole and exclusive path to success, then professors are the gatekeepers of that path. As a result, everything they do takes on a sort of inflated significance, and what's more, some of them like it.

The cold and sterile environment of a classroom or lecture hall isn't very well-suited to most subjects. It's fine to stand a professor in the field of geology up at the front of a class and have her deliver a lecture on the subject, but does anyone really imagine that's what professional geologists do with their time? After a bit of consideration, most realize it isn't. But here we've got the supposed pinnacle of success in the field of geology demonstrating her knowledge with digital slides and a prepared lecture, and grading assignments and exams for her living. Or at least it would appear so.

In actual fact, when professional academia is properly understood, it becomes clear that many professors don't spend all their time in classrooms and offices. Probably that professor of geology does get out into the field at least part of the time. Nonetheless, appearances are powerful, and it still seems as though the height of success, in any field, ends with getting away from the hands-on approach entirely, and moving into an office with ready access to the library. Somewhere along the line, we developed an idea that working in a hands-on way is bad, or lower down on the hierarchy of

When professional academia is properly understood, it becomes clear that many professors don't spend all their time in classrooms and offices.

professional success. We valorize the professionals who work with books and computers and inhabit offices, but we don't have the same respect for anyone who might get dirty on the job. Well, is it any wonder? We're all fed through an education system that takes jobs that might get us dirty, and teaches us all about them in nice clean lecture halls where we learn from nice clean professors who have managed to get away from all that ugly real work. Which isn't fair, naturally, because most professional academics work quite hard. But the surface impression suggests otherwise.

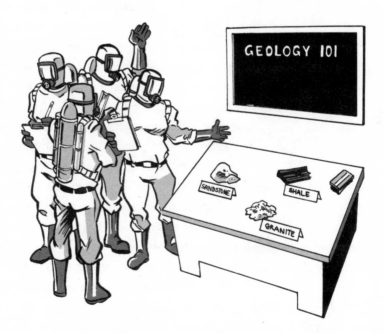

It's another mistake to reduce faculty to the level of service providers. They are very professionally accomplished and deserve respect, and if they are to be impartial toward their students and their research, they need a fair amount of independence. All of this is granted. But it's also dangerous to adopt their lifestyle and their position too fully as a model for success. Some of them have gravitated toward academia as the final expression of a lifetime spent avoiding "real" work. Some of them wield their sense of intellectual superiority as a weapon. Some of them are downright mean and bitter. They're human, just like anyone else. And it's human nature to emphasize the importance of the advantages we personally possess. Academics naturally emphasize the values associated with the lifestyle they've chosen. And that would be fine if we only looked to academics to train and produce other academics. But by turning them into the gatekeepers of all skilled professions and ambitions, we do a major disservice to everyone who imagines any other path in life.

> Academics naturally emphasize the values associated with the lifestyle they've chosen.

I don't think this problem originated with faculty. They are caught in the cycle as much as anyone — both symptom and cause. Many career professors and academics are among the most sensitive and open-minded people I've met. If you ever get a chance to observe your professors closely, however, take a moment to see how they react to the people around them with less professional jobs. See how they behave toward the janitors, the cafeteria staff, and the administrative assistants that support the work of their department. That's a good test of anyone's character.

Salvation in the Classroom

One of the most negative outcomes of the way we've fetishized university is that students, and sometimes their parents, get the strange idea that there's value in being at university even without doing or achieving anything. Students buy their textbooks, then don't read them, but feel as though merely owning them is somehow helpful. They sit in lectures, blank out, or even go to sleep, but still show up every week, comforted by the idea that they're accomplishing something in that way. On the surface, it seems utterly irrational. Why show up constantly to a place where you aren't doing anything useful? Why fool yourself into thinking it's beneficial? Actually there is one other place people have a habit of acting this way. It's church.

Not to make too much of this parallel, but it's fun to think of faculty as the priesthood of academia, and the classroom as the temple. Everything to do with religion gets invested with so much meaning. Not just the locations, but also the implements used, the books, the ceremonies, and everything else. Faith, after all, is a serious business. There's a lot on the line when you're dealing with immortality, salvation, and the other big issues addressed by religion. As a result, even the coat rack where you hang your jacket at the door is invested with meaning. Merely by association there's something desperately important about everything to do with the institution that's devoted to saving your soul.

It would be a mistake to claim that university and education are as important as religion and salvation, but as much as anything mundane *can* compete in importance, then university clearly does so. If religion is all about what's going on beyond this world, then university seems to claim a sort of supreme authority to determine what's going to happen in your present lifetime. If you don't have a university education, you won't be "successful." To many people that's almost as powerful as saying you won't be "saved." As a result, we've got all kinds of strange behaviour going on, as we invest the objects and practices of university with meaning beyond what's rational.

Maybe there's some value in showing up regularly to a place of worship even if you ignore what's being said, and even fall asleep. It isn't for me to say. But I guarantee there's no value to doing so in university. I further guarantee that owning the textbooks conveys no value if you don't read them. Listening to a professor drone on in the background while you think about your significant other won't enlighten you by some process of osmosis. Hanging out in the same building with educated people won't educate you by proximity. All of this is blindingly obvious, of course, but it's still shocking how many students fall into the trap of thinking this way. Less-motivated students find it very attractive to imagine they can get by just going through the motions, but sometimes even engaged students get stuck doing things — just because it's what you *do* — when they don't understand why or what good it is.

> University is not a place and education is not an experience where you can get something out of it by just going through the motions.

And all of this is only possible because university, as an institution, has become sacred.

University is not a place and education is not an experience where you can get something out of it by just going through the motions. Regardless of what you want out of university, it won't happen just because you show up. At most you'll gain some temporary social approval, because from the outside it seems like you're doing something useful. Perhaps that's the main reason why people who aren't otherwise paying any attention show up regularly to their religious institutions too. But that social approval is a dangerous lure. In the case of religion, presumably, the hope is that less-engaged worshippers become more engaged over time. And when parents, teachers, and society in general push their children and students into university for "their own good," it's natural to subtly endorse the value of just showing up. Natural, perhaps, but in the case of university, it's wrong. Students who aren't motivated to be in university shouldn't be there. It's a horrible deception to suggest otherwise.

Terror of Failure

The flip side of wanting success, whatever that means, is fear of failure. Even young people who haven't defined for themselves what success means know for sure they want it, just as they know for sure they don't want to be "failures" in life. And that fear can become very real and powerful. I'd even suggest, as a general rule, that the more students don't really know what they want from university and from life, the more they are motivated by fear rather than desire. All they really have to focus on is what they don't want.

A little bit of fear is natural, even motivating. It's used extensively to "motivate" kids ("just wait until your father/mother gets home!"), but it extends into the adult world as well. Isn't every employee at least a little bit afraid of the boss? So fear is good in moderate quantities. But let's discuss fear of failure at university in the context of a place that's become the begin-all and end-all of success. If there's only one way to succeed in life, and you wipe out there, what's left? You're a failure, that's what. It isn't that you've failed at just one thing. You've failed at everything. Your life might as well be over.

For anyone who has uncritically bought into the idea that university is the one path to success, the fear of failure goes beyond anything that's healthy or motivating, and can become genuine terror. Every once in a while, some expression of this feeling hits the media. Some student kills himself after flunking out of school. Obviously that's horrible, and we all shake our heads and discuss it as a tragedy, but it isn't hard to see where the problem starts. If you condition students to feel as though their lives are over if they can't graduate from university, it isn't so surprising that once in a while someone takes it literally. The problem goes deeper than the occasional tragic story of some kid who took it way too far. You see expressions of this terror all over the place in a modern university.

The students who can't talk with their parents are one example, if not a new one. Kids have been hiding grades from parents for so long it's cliché, so it isn't surprising to see the trend continue in university. But the fear of failure in university is bigger and broader than just a question of family relationships. You'll see students who can't admit to each other they're in trouble. The stigma of failure is so tangible you can almost see students categorizing one another as future doctors, lawyers, or menial workers. And I think we all know how our society values doctors and lawyers, versus manual labourers. It isn't pretty. Sometimes students don't even seek help from the people employed to provide exactly that kind of assistance — because it's too much to admit the problem, even to professional advisors. You see first-year students crushed under the weight of a single bad term, or a single bad year, and even though they aren't suspended or facing any kind of immediate consequences, they just shut down as if they're waiting for the axe to fall. The stamp of failure is already on them. It's awful to see.

These are symptoms of a larger problem. If only we didn't turn university into the alpha and the omega of success in life, there wouldn't be so much pressure on students to succeed. People have different aptitudes, skills, and abilities. Some people take lessons in martial arts and find they aren't very good at it. Some try out for sports teams and can't make the cut. Some try acting, sewing, painting, or sculpting, and find it isn't for them. People "fail" at things all the time without feeling as though their lives are over, or that they are inferior human beings for want of a particular skill. And learning is a skill. Formal education is constructed in such a way that it plays explicitly to certain kinds of talents and aptitudes. Some very worthy people just aren't suited to it. Others could do well in different circumstances, but attend school at the wrong time. Either way, it's absurd and damaging to raise this particular form of endeavour to the point where success or failure at this one thing is the same as success or failure in life. It isn't healthy. And it wouldn't be so bad if it didn't seem as though absolutely everything is determined in this one educational monolith. All the more reason to recognize and legitimize alternative paths to success and achievement in life.

The Scam

When university stops making sense, a certain cynicism sets in. We're all familiar with things that don't make sense, right? Sometimes you just have to go through the motions and fulfill all of the silly requirements in order to accomplish ... whatever. Dealing with the government often feels this way. Why do they need your mother's maiden name, your last place of residence, and form sj-346 filled out in triplicate and signed by a notary public anyway? Ah, who cares. It's just easier to get it done and move on with life. And if the most efficient way to get it done is to fudge around the corners, then it doesn't really matter because the whole thing is contrived and stupid anyway.

Because of their differing priorities, students are continually confronted with requirements that make no sense to them. The vocational student doesn't understand the need for "breadth" requirements that force science students to take English courses and learn poetry. The academic student doesn't understand the need for a standardized playing field, and why she has to do all the same things as everyone else when some other assignment or course work would be so much more interesting. The credential-driven student can't wrap his mind around these participation grades and the group work; he wants to just prove what he knows and get it over with. The list goes on. Those specific examples might not always hold true, but I guarantee that every single student is confronted daily by at least something about university that seems to make no natural sense. More than anything else, it seems like a puzzle to

solve. The prize comes at the end of the maze, but the steps you take to get there don't relate much at all to what you're trying to achieve.

Even at the best of times, it's hard to take instructions and follow through with everything you've been told to do if you don't know why you're doing it. In the case of university, depending on the goals and priorities of individual students, this problem is compounded by the fact that certain things not only seem to make no sense, but in fact *do not* make sense. As a result, many students do exactly what any other intelligent person would do. They know where they are, and they know what they're trying to accomplish, and if there seems to be a far easier and simpler way to get from point A to point B, they take it. In other words, they cheat.

"Beating" the System

I don't want to suggest that lots of students are literally cheating in university in the sense that they are violating academic regulations. Oh, I'm sure some of them are, and I'm also sure that many students cheating today find it far easier to do so because playing by the rules makes no more sense than breaking the rules. But cheating takes a lot of different forms. Some students literally break the rules. Others just circumvent the intent. And an awful lot of students cheat themselves out of the substance of their education.

Forget all that stuff about how cheaters never win. I'm sure lots of students get away with copying work, sharing answers on tests, buying essays, and plagiarizing. It happens all the time. And that's how rumours start. It feeds back into an ugly cycle because as soon as you hear that one person got away with it, the system seems even more broken than it did before. You might as well cheat if everyone else is cheating too. And if you get away with it once, then all bets are off. The problem with straight-up cheating isn't that you'll always be caught. Probably you won't be. But the price you pay when you are caught is massive. Count on it. Cheaters often underestimate how hard the hammer is going to fall, because cheating seemed so normal and natural. Isn't everyone doing it? What happened to a first-time verbal warning, a slap on the wrist? *What do you mean I fail the whole course for a first-time offense and everyone who ever looks at my transcript will know why ... ?!*

Okay, cheating sucks, and I don't want to dwell on

> Forget all that stuff about how cheaters never win.

it. Either don't do it simply because it's wrong, or if you can't manage that, then don't do it because it isn't worth it. Most students understand, or at least think they understand, the rules about cheating and know enough to avoid it. But there's cheating and then there's cheating, right? You'd never try to steal a copy of this year's exam, but maybe if you can score a copy of last year's exam (not intended for release), you'll have an edge. You'd never buy a ready-made essay but if you get your friend to write half of yours for you, then it's sort of like writing it yourself, and anyway, it's uncatchable. And sharing notes with another student on a laboratory assignment isn't really cheating as long as you write separate reports, even if you don't truly understand the experiment you've just conducted.

This kind of halfway cheating leads directly into what I think of as one of the saddest things going on in modern education. Students cheat themselves more than they successfully cheat the system. You might do a little better on tomorrow's exam if you can find out what's going to be on it and study only that material, but when you take the next course, based on a knowledge of this one, you'll pay the price. You might get a friend to help with this essay, or this laboratory section, but what about the next one? And even if you somehow get through university in this way, what are you going to do afterward? Although the connections might be poorly drawn at times, the skills and experience you gain at university genuinely are meant to help you in the real world. Are you going to get a job and rely on your co-workers to cover for you? Not a formula for professional success. Or self-respect, for that matter.

No matter how you slice it, outright cheating is obviously wrong, but when it comes to this kind of halfway cheating, it isn't enough to fault the students because there's a deeper problem here. This attitude was fostered somewhere — the idea that passing the test and getting the grade is more important than learning the material — and I don't think students are to blame. I blame underfunding, I blame cut corners, and I blame an educational system that's succumbed to the economics of scale so much that students are processed more than educated. There are lots of ways that corners get cut, but if you want a concrete example look no further than multiple-choice exams. They've got to be the easiest and cheapest things in the world to grade. As classes get bigger and the cost to hire graders to read through hundreds of papers and exams becomes more and more prohibitive, it's only natural to move to multiple-choice format. It happens in the sciences quickly, then it happens in more qualitative areas like social science, and then it even creeps into the humanities. Multiple-choice test in English? Sure, why not. You can feed a stack of answer sheets through a machine and get them graded in an hour.

The hidden cost of multiple-choice, and other simplified methods of evaluation, isn't that they are ineffective. A well-designed multiple-choice exam can be very accurate at testing students, which is why standard aptitude tests are done this way. It works. But it fosters a dangerous and damaging illusion. When you're staring at five little ovals and the challenge is to fill in the right one, it's very easy to reduce your education to the same challenge. If, at the end of the day, you can pick the right oval, then

all's well with the world. It feels arbitrary and random. Over the course of a hundred such questions, the randomness evens out and students who know the material stand out from those who do not. That's why it works. But the students who take that test, both the good ones and the poor ones, are left with an over-simplified view of education. There's one right answer and four wrong ones, and the goal of education is to know the difference. Just like a game show.

Will This Be on the Exam?

Leaving aside format for a moment, whether multiple-choice or otherwise, let's talk about every instructor's favourite question in the whole world. Picture this scene. The professor has just run through several complicated slides as students scribble madly away. It's a new and difficult topic, and a lot of people look lost. Not only that, but there's a test next week. The professor pauses and invites questions. A dozen hands shoot up immediately. Maybe one or two students want clarification about the ideas that were just introduced. But odds are the great majority of questions are all variations on the same theme. "Will this be on the test?"

I probably don't need to even say this. Everyone knows it isn't consistent with the ideals of education to come right out and ask if something is going to be on the test as though it's the only question that matters. And yet, students also know and acknowledge it's an important question anyway. It would take a very idealistic student, and a naive one, to ignore the question completely. I wouldn't be surprised if students learn with a completely different part of the brain when they know something is going to be on an exam. It's like the extra effort and incentive to remember someone's name, when you've just met them, if you think they're really cute.

I'm not pointing this out to suggest you should stop caring about what's going to be on the test. Hell, I care about what's going to be on the test. But I think it's important to realize that we all approach university and education with a bit of a dual perspective, and it isn't healthy. On the one hand, we appreciate that we are there to learn certain things or gain certain kinds of certification in order to go on to do what we want with our lives, and the information itself, removed from any kind of evaluation, is important. On the other hand, we know the grades will matter, and that there are tricks and tactics to score the grades. And so we use them. Even at the best of times, it's a game we're out to beat. So I won't advise you ignore this fact. Just keep your attempts to beat the system on the right side of academic regulations, and remember that some ideas of how to beat the system are self-defeating. There still isn't such a thing as an easy course, no matter what that guy in the back row says. Why listen to him? He's sleeping half the time anyway.

The Man

The sense that university is just a scam, that success is something you trick your way into, rather than earn on the basis of talent and hard work, extends beyond just methods of evaluation and grading. There seems to be something scammy about the whole thing. Students feel screwed a lot of the time, right? And for good reasons if you ask me. So it's no wonder so many feel as though something shady is going on. Maybe you can't quite put your finger on it, but it definitely feels as though they're out to get you. This situation is messed up and it isn't accidental. Surely someone is benefitting from it. "They" know they're ripping you off, and they're doing it deliberately.

I'm not trying to sound absurd here; I'm just repeating things I've heard from genuinely distressed students who want to know what's happened to their education. And those students spend an awful lot of time talking about what "they" are doing, or have done, or might do. I'm not entirely sure what "they" those students mean, and I doubt they know either. Sometimes I think it's faculty who are implicated; quite often it's the administration; sometimes it's the government. Once in a while, student representatives and organizations such as unions and councils are included in the lump category of "them." I've had it directed at me sometimes. Anything and anyone that's part of "the system" is suspect. The point is that students are disappointed, and it seems as though someone must be to blame, so they refer freely to "them," the people who are to blame, without worrying too much about who "they" are.

> If you're out to blame someone specific, then find out who's at fault, and say so. But don't blame "them."

If something sucks and you can find out who is to blame, then blame that person. Please note that it's often reductive to just blame the professor standing in front of the classroom. If you discuss the things you dislike with your professors, you might be pleasantly surprised at all the information and suggestions you receive. That's a side note. The major point is that if you're out to blame someone specific, then find out who's at fault, and say so. But don't blame "them." That's just lazy and irrational. It's another way of saying you're feeling cheated, but can't figure out what happened. And that's a good thing to say also, if it's how you feel, but you might as well be honest about what you don't know. Directing your complaints at an abstract "they" won't change anything. You've got to call out your targets.

Hopefully, armed with this book and a greater sense of the various players and pressures at work in university, you'll be able to direct your complaints at specific people when you need to. That alone certainly won't solve any problems in your life, but it's a good first step. Sometimes it might be impossible to blame one particular person or group of people. Some problems are simply inherent in the system: they're either no one's fault, or possibly everyone's fault. And we still need a way to complain about that. It's too natural to avoid it.

So blame it on The Man. There used to be a great tradition about blaming The Man, and sometimes stickin' it to The Man, that unfortunately went out of style. We need to bring it back. Because it really is important to express the concept, every once in a while, that we feel the deck is stacked against us. A certain irrationality is built right into blaming The Man, but it's hanging out there for everyone to see. We all know there isn't a literal "man" out to get us. But it sure does feel like there might be anyway, doesn't it?

The generation that's running things these days, and making most of the decisions that affect our lives, knows all about The Man. He was messing with them all the way back in the '70s. And they know what you mean when you blame The Man. It isn't just about someone who is directly out to get you — it's also about all the people in positions of authority who might be able to make things better if they cared enough to bother, but they don't. It's about neglect and ignorance as much as anything else. Call them on it! Decades ago they knew what it felt like. They used to say, "Don't trust anyone over thirty." Force them to confront the question of what they aren't doing to help you, rather than what they may or may not have done to actually harm you.

The Man doesn't want you to think too carefully about all this. He'd rather have you just continue to talk about "them" and stop there, because you think you've said something coherent. Don't let The Man keep you down!

Further

When students are heading into their final years of high school there aren't many who are concerned about graduating. Most of them know they're going to graduate. The real question is what they'll be able to do after graduation. Everyone wants to know what it will take to get into university or what it will take to get into college. Perhaps some students have given up on their prospects, they're resigned to simply graduate and move on with life. But it seems rather odd, if you think about it, that nearing the end of this particular challenge, almost no one is worried about whether or not they can finish. The real question is who can go *further*.

This experience is repeated at the undergraduate level, and becomes, if anything, more pronounced. Even before students arrive and begin their first-year classes, some of them are already asking about professional and graduate programs. What do I need to get into law school? What will guarantee me a place in teachers' college? What are the minimum grades to get accepted into graduate school? Leaving aside the fact that absolute answers to these questions are almost impossible, since the requirements are different everywhere and cut-offs shift each year, there's something fascinating about the fact that students aren't at all concerned about finishing their degrees (at least not before they get into trouble), but are focused, rather, on worrying about their positions at the end of the degree and whether or not they'll be able to go *further*.

Some might claim that students have just missed the point by asking these questions and getting so worried about the future, but the reality on the ground supports their view. What's the major difference between a high-school graduate who just barely scraped by with passing grades, and one with an average in the high '90s? You won't find many employers who are going to care about your high-school grades, so the obvious difference is simply that the latter student will have a wide range of options about further education while the former won't have many. And the same holds true for a graduate with a bachelor's degree. Sad to say, but many employers do not take the time or trouble to be informed about grades, or to obtain reliable information about them. So the difference between a graduate with a C average versus an A average? You guessed it — it's still the same deal. The A student can go on to professional or graduate school and the C student is about to enter the workforce. But if the A student wants to enter the workforce anyway, both are on more or less equal footing, at least in terms of their degrees. Doesn't seem fair, does it? Well, fair is a relative concept. But for sure it isn't efficient.

A Service to (Lazy) Industry

If the certification function of education is primarily a service to industry, and a means to help the economy, you'd think that industry could at least take the trouble to use all available information. But this isn't the case. A lot of the time, industry (employers) won't bother to figure out the difference between a good high-school graduate and a poor one, or someone who did well as an undergraduate versus someone who did less well. I would never claim that success in school (or lack of it) tells the entire tale about the potential of an employee, but if employers want this kind of information, you'd think they'd at least take it. Instead they take the lazy way out.

> The one sure way to tell a good high-school student is to find someone who has a bachelor's degree.

If the major difference between a good high-school student and a poor one is the ability to go to university, then the one sure way to tell a good high-school student is to find someone who has a bachelor's degree. Similarly, if you want to find a good undergraduate student, you look for someone with a graduate or professional degree, and so on. And this really does occur. Students have bought into the concept; employers have bought into the concept; and educational institutions (never unwilling to expand) have gladly gone along for the ride. I'm not suggesting that everyone is doing this consciously, but if you think about the way various degrees and qualifications are considered, you'll see this is happening. And so the debt piles up while students struggle to gain credentials in order to prove what was already obvious from their previous performance, if anyone could be bothered to consult or credit the evidence already at hand.

Anyone Who Gets In ...

One of the best mantras of guidance counsellors and academic advisors is something like "If you were good enough to get in here, then you're good enough to graduate." And it's actually quite true. That isn't to say students don't fail or flunk out entirely, but the educational system in Canada isn't built on the premise that a sizable portion of students needs to fail at any particular level. Any system needs a process to weed students out, but the Canadian educational system, on the whole, weeds out students at the application stage. So advisors are quite justified in saying, "If you got in, you can graduate." The real question for most students, after all, isn't whether they can graduate, but what their standing will be when they do.

Advisors are quite justified in saying, "If you got in, you can graduate."

In one sense, this is encouraging news, which is exactly why guidance counsellors repeat the information so frequently. If you're struggling, and you aren't sure whether university is for you, then you're justified in telling yourself that you've passed the major hurdle already. If you were admitted, then you should, at least, have the raw ability to graduate. You might not be motivated or enthusiastic enough to do so, and these are issues to address, but there's no rule built into the system that demands a certain portion of students must fail. If you apply yourself diligently, you should be able to graduate. So if that's your goal, take heart! From an institutional standpoint, however, this is a pretty poor system. It burdens many students with needless debt, and years of education they may not need.

There are, as I've said, many good reasons to get post-secondary education. Certainly there's a social good, if nothing else, to educating more and more young people in Canada. But from the perspective of an individual who just wants to prove general ability in order to get a job, this is a horrible system. An undergraduate degree, after four years of expensive education, proves that a student was good in high school and then spent four more years exercising a reasonable degree of diligence and dedication. That much could be established with just a look at the same student's high-school transcript and a few weeks of on-the-job evaluation. The same points reoccur when graduate and professional degrees are required to prove general competence. For those students who need specialized training, the point is different, of course, but it's becoming increasingly axiomatic that a large proportion of students are not working in their areas of education at all, and just used their degrees to get their feet in various doors.

Is this the best way we could offer education in Canada? For those seeking to emerge with the best qualifications in the least amount of time, and with the least debt possible, it would be far kinder to promote a system of evaluation able to separate good from bad students at an earlier stage, if only to save everyone time and expense.

CHAPTER SIX

THE BIG INVESTMENT

Financial Pressure

It's almost impossible to talk about post-secondary education today without confronting the issue of cost. I know I've mentioned it many times already, but the full influence of rising tuition can't really be described — it must be felt. If you're a student in university today, or contemplating it, I know you've felt it. Even if you're independently wealthy, I'm sure you can feel the influence on the students around you. The difference between high school and university is not merely in atmosphere or difficulty; there's a far deeper distinction that everyone senses, even if they can't quite put words to it. High school is just something you do. You take it for granted in much the same way you take for granted a trip to the doctor (in Canada, anyway), with all the confidence that it's simply there for you.

University is different. It isn't something you just use; it's something you have to buy. Some enjoy the privilege of parents who can pay for it out of pocket. Others work their asses off in order to pay for it personally. Many go into debt. It's an investment, and a big one.

The monetary cost of education creates a corresponding atmosphere of seriousness. It's bloody hard to spend thousands of dollars every term and not think about where it's going. Some students react with feelings of discontent and resentment. Some simply take the cost of education and put an equivalent amount of pressure on themselves to succeed. And many students look at the bills as they accumulate, and start to think very seriously about how they are going to go out and earn money. Maybe they need to pay back the government, their parents, or the bank. Maybe they just have to justify, in some material way, the cost of the education. But after years of time and tens of thousands of dollars, that degree had really better pay off.

This situation is not positive. Students who feel screwed and resentful are poorer students, and they risk missing out on the very education that's costing them so much. Students who dwell too much on the pressure and obligations weighing down on them are just asking for problems and breakdowns. A little bit of pressure can be motivating, sure, but when students start lying to their families, and refusing to face problems they are experiencing, it's clearly unhealthy. Every guidance office is familiar with stories of this kind. And those students who search too desperately for ways to cash in on their degrees are susceptible to all the issues associated with the career motive. Some are led naturally toward their interests and inclinations, and find ways to pursue related jobs, and that's well and good for them. But other students, either less lucky or acting on poorer advice, get trapped playing away from their strengths and interests in hopes of finding secure careers. This rarely ends well. The cost of education is not merely an unfortunate burden on students and their families, but is actually skewing the very practice of it.

No Ordinary Deal

In Canada, we've got contract law that makes it impossible for a minor to sign a binding legal agreement under ordinary circumstances, but that doesn't apply in the case of education, according to long-standing legal precedent.[1] Just in case precedent isn't sufficient, the government has made it explicit in the Canada Student Loans Act that age is no barrier to long-term debt; children are just as liable for it.[2] We've also got bankruptcy laws that govern how deeply in debt you can get without hope of recovery, and how you can get out of it, but those laws are stacked against students with special provisions written directly into the Bankruptcy and Insolvency Act.[3] It is clear, in numerous ways, that where our laws are concerned, education is no ordinary deal. Rather it seems like the exception to every rule.

Although you cannot normally, at the age of sixteen or seventeen, sign yourself into a binding contract, that rule goes right out the window when it comes to student debt. When you accept a government loan, it's your loan, you are responsible for it, and that's just it. You can't get a credit card, sign a cellular phone contract, or anything else, but you can sign yourself into thousands upon thousands of dollars of debt if it's for education. You aren't considered old enough to drink, buy cigarettes, vote,

or make personal decisions about all kinds of other things in your life, but you are considered old enough and responsible enough to commit your income and finances toward paying a debt that might last into your thirties, or beyond.

The other side of student debt is even nastier. You can become bankrupt because you utterly failed to manage your spending habits. You can go bankrupt because you invested heavily in a shady business venture that might have made you rich but didn't. Regardless of how or why you went into debt, with *very* few exceptions, you can always declare bankruptcy, and the rules are basically the same. Your credit rating will plummet, and years will pass before anyone will trust you with any kind of loan or long-term contract again, but you'll get a clean slate, and you will be able to start rebuilding your life.

Unless, of course, you took out a government loan in order to pay for your education. In that case you'll have to wait ten years from the point at which you finished school before you can declare bankruptcy, and then you'll only be at the beginning of a process that is already long and difficult.

So there seems to be a value judgment and a pattern of logic here. First, the government has determined that even young people — who aren't considered able to make other responsible decisions in life — *are* able to decide to go into debt for their education. Presumably that's because a decision to invest in education can never be the wrong decision, though I would love to argue that point with any legislator who might try to defend it. Second, the government has determined that education is so special, and such a good investment, that those who buy it are not allowed to declare bankruptcy in the usual way. So is this true? Is it simply impossible to go wrong in purchasing your education — so much so that even a child (legally speaking) is allowed to buy one? And is it such a sure investment that bankruptcy should never be an issue until a full decade later?

In answer to the idea that no one, even a legal minor, can make a "wrong" decision to buy education, I'll simply say the argument is absurd. Even insulting. Many students attend university or college at the wrong time. Others go to the wrong place. Even adults, in later life, second-guess their decisions and make bad choices. Yet we act as though this one financial decision, this one investment, is so clearly the "right" choice that we bend all our social values, and ideas about who is and isn't responsible enough to make these choices, to allow it. It's further proof that we are so obsessed with education, as a society, that it trumps all our other values.

In terms of later finances, of course students end up broke, poor, and saddled with massive debt after graduation. Or at least some do. But they don't have access to the same chance to start over as others have. There are those who will say that education can't be repossessed, and that's part of the logic behind this rule. The principles of bankruptcy, after all, say you can't go out and buy an expensive car, then declare you're broke. They'll take the car back first. But you can't give back an education. We all know that. It's part of the deal. But you also can't give back many of the experiences and opportunities that relate to other kinds of debt. Declaring bankruptcy implies that you screwed up somehow, or at least had horrible luck. What about those students who took a chance on education, and found it didn't pay off? Don't they deserve at least as much of an opportunity to start over as someone who took a chance at entrepreneur-ship, even in a risky area?

> Our bankruptcy laws have tighter rules on education not because it's impossible to screw up the investment, but rather because it's so easy to do so.

It's transparently false that students shouldn't need to declare bankruptcy because they all earn a lot of money with their degrees and diplomas. For some people, it works exactly that way and it's a good deal. Others struggle. And some plunge into impossible financial situations. Our bankruptcy laws have tighter rules on education not because it's impossible to screw up the investment, but rather because it's so easy to do so. If students were allowed to go bankrupt on their student loans the way that anyone else can declare bankruptcy, it would probably be so common the federal and provincial budgets would need to be redesigned to account for it. This isn't because university students are stupid, or lazy, and it isn't because they have any greater desire to slaughter their credit ratings than anyone else. It's because investment in higher education is just like any other investment. Sometimes it doesn't pay off.

Here's a lie built right into our legal system. On the one hand, we imply that even a child should be able to invest responsibly and successfully in education. It's that sure a thing. On the other hand, we stack the deck against those same children after they've graduated (assuming they graduate), because we're terrified of what might happen if students who can't pay back their loans had a way out, even a way as ugly as bankruptcy. So which is it?

Taxation, Now or Later

Here in Canada, we've got a basic idea going on that says those with greater opportunities and greater wealth pay more of the cost to sustain our very fortunate and privileged society. We all argue back and forth about just how much more the people who can pay should pay, and about how it should be calculated, and about what kind of system works best, but almost no one disputes the basic premise: those who are able to pay more should pay more.

There is a natural correlation between greater education and higher income. This becomes part of the argument to justify the cost. In this respect, it's a lot like taxation. The cost of education is put on the shoulders of everyone who attends school with the hope that they will subsequently go off and become, in relative terms, high earners. Taxation, in contrast, is put primarily on the shoulders of everyone who is actually earning a better-than-average living. At least that's the theory, and one hopes our system functions as intended, that those more able to pay do, in fact, shoulder the greater share of the cost.

The rising cost of education is nothing other than a pay-in-advance form of taxation — for something that is undeniably good for the individual and also good for the economy in general, and for society at large. It's not at all a sure thing, especially with regards to personal earning potential. Even the students who graduate with degrees aren't guaranteed opportunities to put them to work, and there are inevitably causalities along the way who don't graduate at all, emerging from university with no credentials other than loan documents to show for it.

This book isn't meant to be a political tract, and I apologize if I seem to promote a political agenda on this point, but I'd like all students and prospective students to consider the sort of contract they sign when they buy education in Canada. Your education is an investment. You're going to hear that a lot. But the actual institutions that provide it have no stake in making sure it's a successful investment, and the government that is underwriting the cost of your education is so uncertain about your ability to realize an effective return, that it has slanted all the normal rules of investment against you so that you can't bail out.

The obvious alternative is a more normal form of taxation. If the government was so certain that greater education would translate into greater income, it could simply tax that income in the future. Perhaps that seems unfair to those who achieve high income without higher education, or those who seek their education outside of the country. One alternative is to fund education properly and centrally, but also to move those who take advantage of the opportunity into a higher bracket as future taxpayers. Variations on the tax system are certainly possible but the basic issue is this — a government that asks its students to pay a big-ticket price for education, upfront, has no real confidence in the long-term value of that education. They'll swear it's a good investment, and produce evidence to prove it works out (at least for the majority of students), but at the end of the day, you assume all the risk.

Education versus Health Care

Students often get angry about the cost of their education, wonder what's wrong with the system, and why there isn't more money. That's such a big question that it deserves a book all to itself, but if you're in university or will be soon, I'd encourage you to take some economics or political science courses to learn more about these issues. In the short term, I'll just discuss a quirk of the Canadian economy that has a lot of influence on the cost of your education.

Way back when the original colonies that now comprise Canada were first negotiating a combined federal government, they had to settle a few questions regarding local (provincial) authority and central (federal) authority. It's a natural enough issue and I'm sure it involved some complex discussion, but the

WHAT'S WRONG WITH UNIVERSITY

essential question came down to, "Who is in charge of what?" Provinces retained control of various issues and expenses that were deemed to be largely local concerns. An arrangement that continues to this day, these include education and health care.

From a modern perspective, it is surprising to realize this, but when Canada was formed neither education nor health care were big-ticket items, in terms of government spending. It made sense to leave them in the hands of the provinces because central authority wasn't needed. Along with control of these areas comes the right to raise taxes to pay for them. And because of these very pragmatic decisions, a major tension exists today regarding how to fund both education and health care.

A massive portion of the total budget, in each province, goes into the combination of health care and education. The room to maneuver around these two priorities is relatively slight. As much as people hate to admit it (especially politicians, who need to worry about appearances), any discussion around funding health care raises the ugly prospect of taking money away from education, and any discussion of funding education brings up the nasty suggestion of raiding the health-care budget. The alternative, of course, is to simply raise taxes. But if that option is rejected, and everyone is scrambling to grab for a bigger piece of the existing pie, it's impossible to deny it has to come from somewhere else. And the biggest pieces, by far, belong to these two areas.

I don't know if it's possible to find a "right" and a "wrong" in this equation, but with an aging population in Canada, it's natural, even obvious, that health care has been consuming more and more of

this limited budget. University administrators aren't blind to this, and Dr. Carolyn Tuohy has even termed this an issue of "intergenerational equity," which is a tactful way to observe that one generation is getting the short end of the stick.[4] The baby-boom generation, which has had its way politically for decades and continues to get its way with voting power and lobbying clout, is getting all the tax dollars. The money was in education when they needed education, and now it's in health care when they need health care. So it isn't fair, in any objective sense, and the younger generations today deserve to be angry. Except it's hard to cry "foul!" when your grandmother needs her hip replaced. And that's exactly why you just about never hear the question of educational funding phrased in these terms. No one wants to admit we have finite resources, and that the health-care needs of one generation are in competition with the educational needs of another generation. But that's what's happening.

There are no easy answers here, but if you believe, as I do, that the needs of younger Canadians deserve as much attention as anyone else's, it's vital to express yourself politically. If you want to take back some of the power, then get involved and encourage your fellow students to get involved. The simplest way to start is to go out and vote each election. No matter who you choose to support, and even if you don't have strong attachments to any party or cause, the more a population demographic votes, the more politicians are obliged to consider what that demographic wants. So vote, and get your fellow students voting. We don't all agree on what we want out of university, and we aren't likely to agree on any single social agenda, so I'm not going to push a particular cause or political perspective. Make up your own mind there. But unless you want to blindly trust that people who don't share your reality today are going to make the best decisions for you, it's worthwhile to remind them you're watching.

Silencing Dissent

Universities are full of creative young minds with the potential to do things no one has done before, to think of things no one has thought of before, and maybe change our world for the better. We all recognize the power of education and its potential to generate change, to shake up society, and maybe to save us from some of the problems we've made for ourselves. When we're faced with problems that seem to have no solutions (no need to list them, they appear in the papers daily), we console ourselves with the belief that something new will come along and somehow fix things. And maybe that belief is justified, to a point, because humans are nothing if not creative. Somewhere, surely, among the many talented young students, there's the next great idea. But that idea will never see the light of day if all those students rush in and out of university, and go straight to work the way they've been told. True creativity involves dissent; it involves disagreement with the established order of things. And today that disagreement comes at a very high price.

I've talked about how the cost of education skews the way students approach their university experience, and how it affects their choices and priorities. Undeniably, students are focusing more and more on educational choices that can pay off in hard dollars and cents. But beyond even the issue of what students are learning, and how they approach their studies, there's the matter of what they are doing when they graduate. Are they challenging the assumptions and the accepted standards of society? Are they taking risks and exploring new ground? Or are they out looking for the best, most secure jobs possible, so they can get right down to paying for their very expensive education?

I doubt there is any way to measure what I'm getting at here, but common sense can prove the point. Graduates today don't have any room to screw around. Many students dream about backpacking around Europe for a few weeks (or some equivalent), and hopefully those who plan it right even get their graduation trips abroad, but after that, it's down to business. Whether driven by debt, or a need to validate the savings and sacrifices of parents, or even (for the wealthy few) just a general sense of the seriousness of education, it seems almost obligatory that once you have the degree, you put it right to work in some conventional way. Imagine trying to justify anything else to your family and friends. Obviously, once you are done with school, you go out and get a "real" job. Otherwise why were you there in the first place?

If many students end up in university simply by following the herd and adhering to expectations, the same thing can occur after graduation. Students move through the educational arms race until they just can't compete anymore, and then take their bachelors' degrees, professional degrees, designations and diplomas, Ph.D.'s, whatever, and they go out to get whatever kinds of jobs they can to justify it all. Maybe most of those people are happy with their jobs, and with their lives. It isn't for me to judge them one way or the other. But I do think we need to worry about the general situation if that's the only option. What about real creativity, after all? What about the kind of dissent that starts out by rejecting the safe path and received assumptions? Is there any place for that attitude at all?

The Alchemy of Youth

The '60s have been glamourized almost to the point that it's hard to get at the reality of the time. It was an important decade, for sure, but there's no sense in romanticizing the whole hippie thing to the point that we lose sight of what was really going on. Most of those long-haired bums were just looking for a good excuse to sit around, avoid real work as much as possible, smoke dope, have sex, and listen to their music. Which actually sounds pretty good, doesn't it? Maybe we've all been there to at least some degree, or wished we could be. But it isn't something we want to encourage or endorse. At most it's just a "phase" we go through before coming to our senses and "growing up." We all know the rhetoric so well, we don't even need our parents to tell us these things anymore — we tell them to ourselves. We know you can't really live like that, and the vast majority of the long-haired hippies learned the same thing. So sure, it's a phase. But maybe there's more to it than storing up anecdotes to prove to your kids that you weren't always boring. Maybe that phase matters, not just to the teenager or twentysomething who wants to have some fun before he has to grow up and get a real job, but to society.

Underneath all the stories, the politics, and the cultural shifts of the '60s and '70s, there's the basic fact that people were thinking new things, and trying out new ways of living as a society. Rochdale College, associated with the University of Toronto, is one famous example of an alternative approach to both living and learning.[5] Now, let's be honest here, ninety-eight percent of this experimentation failed badly, and perhaps was doomed to failure. But the remaining two percent contained ideas that are still at work today. It was a formative time, so it's no wonder we look back on it as a fateful period, something that was somehow destined to happen. But that same kind of thing is going on all the time. People challenge the way we live as a society all the

time. People question what we're doing, and why we're doing it. The whole hippie movement, flower power and all the rest of it, was a concentrated dose of creative dissent, but the tradition of questioning and challenging assumptions goes back as far as recorded history. It's a part of how we learn.

If you're worried that I'm about to call for some return to barefoot revolution, you can rest easy, because I'm not. I'd just like to point out how impossible it all seems now. To actually drop out of society, either before, during, or after education is almost unthinkable. But it's the very fact that it's becoming unthinkable that indicates there's a real problem. Change has to come from somewhere. We all acknowledge there are huge problems in the world today — social, economic, environmental, and political. So we can't imagine the best thing possible is to just put our heads down, and keep going on as we have been, right? Some people place their faith in grey-haired politicians and mysterious scientists to find the magic that's going to save us from ourselves. Personally, I'd rather trust some homeless punk with a skateboard, because at least she's free enough to really think about things.

Youth is glamourized so much by the media that it's awkward to point this out, but there genuinely is something special about being young. Perhaps it has more to do with lifestyle and social circumstance than anything else, but young people often have the freedom to do things older people simply can't do. When you don't have a mortgage, a family to support, or a particular reason why you're confined to one place of residence or one lifestyle, well, that's a kind of freedom. And not surprisingly, this is where change comes from. When you can stand outside of some of the assumptions of society, and look at things directly, you have a perspective older people simply can't share. For the vast majority of people, this is a phase they grow out of quickly. And probably as people get older, they find that most of the things they didn't like before make a lot more sense from a different viewpoint, and this is all normal and natural. But change does happen, and even though the push for change may eventually move through the expected channels of politics and the mainstream media, does it actually start there? Where does the spark come from in the first place, and where did the idea first arise? This is a large philosophical question, but a relevant one.

As we talk about education as an investment in the future, we need to remember that we're talking about a future that must look different from today. The investment is a poor one if we take the products of education, and our creative young minds, and simply harness them to the same old engines. It isn't a matter of filling those minds with knowledge and sending them off to "be successful," it's a matter of giving them room to question the validity of what they've learned, and maybe even question the accepted standards of success their parents are so certain about. There's no way to institutionalize opportunities to question institutions, so the only option is to just leave our teenagers and early twentysomethings alone for a while. Just give them a bit of space. Seems simple, doesn't it? But it's also apparently the hardest thing imaginable to many people. Everyone is so eager to tell students and young people what they should be doing, that they forget to ask what they want to do, or sometimes even what they think about it all.

The Hidden Cost of Cost

There are many side effects to high-cost education. The authorities that defend such things generally acknowledge the effects as unfortunate but unavoidable. High costs are treated as a natural outgrowth of the modern age, and something we simply have to live with. The cost is usually justified, on the level of macroeconomics, by pointing to indicators that prove an educated workforce is good for the economy. And no doubt that's true. But hopefully we can all agree there is more to a healthy society than a roaring economy. Not only do we value things other than material wealth alone (or I sure hope so), we also admit that we need to come up with better ways of living. And sometimes I wonder who's going to do that if we so directly indoctrinate all our bright young people into the social, political, and economic assumptions of the present day that they never have time to imagine how things could be different.

When a student has tens of thousands of dollars of debt, that isn't a short-term obligation. It's a lifestyle. That young man or woman is going to be more than thirty, in all likelihood, before the debt is cleared. By that time, there will be car payments, mortgage obligations, family expenses, perhaps even retirement savings! Whatever window once existed for that person to question society, to grapple creatively with the assumptions of the majority, has been lost. Probably most of us can move through life and never even realize we've lost that chance. But at some point, society as a whole will feel the cost. Not in something that we've lost, but in something that we've never even found. That new idea that might have made things better just never arrives.

There are ways you can take control of your experience in university, push it beyond the cookie-cutter standard, perhaps explore some ideas and options you'd otherwise miss, and I'll provide some suggestions in Chapter Eight. But I still believe that for a single young adult, minimum wage is far more liberating, in many ways, than a high-priced education. When you're debt-free, you can still move in any direction. Post-secondary education is a long-term decision, however, that will exclude other options.

> When a student has tens of thousands of dollars of debt, that isn't a short-term obligation. It's a lifestyle.

You aren't wrong to be in university, if you are already. It isn't a mistake to go there either, if you know what you want. Just please don't lose sight of the things you've missed to do it. It's tempting to write off the value of choices we've passed up, so that we don't have to deal with any regrets. But you never know when you might need to reconsider your choices, and when the ambitions that once seemed so important to you might not make as much sense anymore. If you blind yourself to other options, you'll only forget they exist at all. And worse, one day you might find yourself teaching your kids the same thing.

1 In the 1925 case, *Millar v. Smith and Co.*, the ruling states an "infant may bind himself to pay for his necessary meat, drink, clothing, medicines, and likewise for his teaching or instruction." That's a pretty radical view, but it has been upheld in practice since.

2 The Canada Student Loans Act reads, "A guaranteed student loan made by a lender to a borrower not of full age [...] is recoverable by the lender from the borrower as though the borrower had been of full age at the time the loan was made." It doesn't get more explicit than that.

3 Section 178 of the Bankruptcy and Insolvency Act reads, "An order of discharge does not release the bankrupt from [...] any debt or obligation in respect of a loan made under the Canada Student Loans Act, the Canada Student Financial Assistance Act [...] within ten years after the date on which the bankrupt ceased to be a full- or part-time student."

4 Carolyn Tuohy is a professor at the University of Toronto, specializing in public policy. Her comments regarding "intergenerational equity" are in context of the university's submission to the Rae Review, with which she was heavily involved as vice-president responsible for policy development.

5 Rochdale College operated between 1968 and 1975. Though a source of considerable controversy, there's no denying it was successful in many ways, and had lasting impact on the cultural and intellectual fabric of both Toronto and Canada. Numerous memoirs, articles, and stories have been written on the subject.

CHAPTER SEVEN

PROPOSALS FOR REFORM

A Few Modest Suggestions

The primary point of this book, all along, has been to help students get the most out of university as it exists today. We might all wish things could be different, and we probably don't agree on the exact changes we'd like to see, but every student has to cope with the reality in the meanwhile. Still, it also helps to have some goal or idea in sight that might improve things. So this chapter will offer ideas.

I'm not even going to pretend I have a road map for how these proposed reforms could be made real. There's no current movement to join, and no mailing list to sign up for if you like any of this stuff. Even if someone came along and made me Minister of Education at a provincial or federal level, I wouldn't be able to do this alone. It takes a major social shift to see changes of this nature. But it has to start somewhere, and if any of these ideas get you talking to your fellow students, then I'm glad to have done that much.

The natural connection between this chapter and the last one is simply the power of an idea. If you believe, as I do, that it's important for university education to generate discussion, and inquiry about our society, then university itself is as important a subject as any — perhaps a more important subject than most. It's also a fun topic to talk about with other students, because it's the one thing you're sure to have in common.

Redefine "Of Age"

I've said before, and I'll say again, that the government is cheating when it comes to student debt. Teenagers who aren't old enough to sign any other binding contract are able to sign themselves into a decade or more of debt. "Kids" who aren't considered responsible enough to buy a bottle of beer are expected to know what they want to do with the rest of their lives — or at least to know well enough to spend tens of thousands of dollars on it. University students who aren't able to vote, in many cases, for the government of the day are increasingly on the losing side of funding decisions about which they've had no say. This kind of double standard is beyond simply unfair, it's downright absurd.

Discussion about the age of majority and the legal age to do anything else in society is always a hot topic. There are movements underway to lower the voting age to sixteen, just as there are movements in various provinces to lower the drinking age. There are also movements to raise the age for various activities including not only drinking, but also driving, consensual sex, smoking, or any number of other things. All of these are interesting debates unto themselves, and I don't want to get into a discussion regarding the consequences of sex, drinking, or the nature of an informed voter. The only point I'd like to make is that one is either a responsible adult, or one isn't. And we've got a lot of conflicting standards on this subject.

As far as I'm concerned, anyone who is old enough to attend higher education, and to sign a government loan document should be old enough to drink, vote, drive, gamble, participate in any form of consensual sexual activity, own a firearm, sign every other form of contract, and hold government office.

Obviously not all at the same time. I'm not entirely sure what that age should be. We've got fifteen- and sixteen-year-old students in university today. Fifteen is highly unusual, but sixteen is simply uncommon. Seventeen is well within the range of what's now considered "normal." Is that old enough to make life-changing decisions? Perhaps not. But if that's the case, let's talk about a common standard. And if it is old enough, then let the kids vote, and get drunk once in a while. It's the least we can do for them, since many won't be out of debt until their thirties.

The debate around the appropriate age to engage in any activity will always be deeply influenced by social values. When we talk about the legal age to engage in sex, we aren't just talking about responsible decision-making; we're also talking about what we think of sex. Similarly, when we talk about drinking, smoking, or driving, all of our opinions on those subjects crowd in, and we can't focus exclusively on what age is old enough to make a responsible choice. Maybe there's something to that. Maybe some decisions are more serious than others, and an awareness of this fact has to be part of our system. But in that case, let's be honest about what we're doing.

If fifteen or sixteen isn't old enough to make responsible adult decisions, a principle that's reflected in many of our laws, and if we have students at fifteen or sixteen in our universities and colleges accumulating student debt, and we do, then there's a basic truth we need to confront. Someone has made that decision for them. Parents, counsellors, society as a whole, take your pick. Our society has become so convinced — I might even say obsessed — regarding the value of higher education that our laws support a system that takes young people who are commonly held to not be responsible for their decisions and places them in debt that might take them a decade or more to clear. And we insist that we're doing it for their own good. But that is, and must remain, their decision to make. Either they are old enough to make it, or they aren't.

I propose a legal minimum age to enter higher education, and that all other legal age limits be changed to adhere to that same standard. If that creates wholesale social reform, and makes parents and legislators uncomfortable, that's just great. The image of a sixteen-year-old kid driving down to the local voting station, then stopping off at the corner pub for a beer and a smoke is a scary one. But that same kid just signed a government loan. And we owe him some answers.

Separation of Functions

The most obvious response to my points about the competing interests and intentions (academic learning, citizenry, vocational training, certification, holding pen) in higher education would be to somehow separate the functions, and create different institutions devoted to more specific goals. Of course that has been tried in the past, and some institutions exist as testimony to this. Somehow an effort to separate functions never works quite as intended. There seems to be a sort of gravitational force at work that keeps pulling the functions back together.

The most obvious and traditional example is college, where you go to get vocational training. To an extent that distinct function still exists, but it's under challenge all the time. Universities are moving more and more toward directed vocational degrees, and colleges frequently offer the sorts of general arts education that isn't employment driven except in the widest sense.

The CEGEP Model and Transfer Agreements

Quebec has an interesting take on this problem with a college system that takes the place of pre-university. It's called CEGEP, which (in English) stands for College of General and Vocational Education. These institutions host both vocational (technical) programs and pre-university programs. Prior to undergraduate university students attend two years at CEGEP, with fairly broad educational content, before continuing toward a more narrow focus in later studies. This becomes the first stage of post-secondary education, so that the subsequent university degree (if a student continues) is shorter. Because it's focused entirely on teaching, this education is less expensive than university, and allows students to keep their options open. It also benefits from better funding than most other provinces in Canada provide for post-secondary schooling. Maybe Quebec is on to something. If nothing else, they've found a clear and distinct role for colleges.

For students who are looking for some basic certification of their competence, the CEGEP system is, in my mind, perfect. It allows students to pursue their education in a way that isn't stigmatized, but it also doesn't dump them directly into university as the one thinkable choice. For holding-pen students, well, I still think that people who have no reason to pursue (and pay for) post-secondary education should wait until they're sure of what they want to do. But at least CEGEP provides these students with a less expensive and less painful way to sort themselves out.

CEGEP is, in some ways, the full expression of an idea that does appear in other contexts. Universities will apply transfer credits toward their degrees for students who have already attended college. Unfortunately this system is haphazard, and every university uses individual systems of assessment, and sets internal policies regarding how to credit college experience. So students never know what to expect, and can't use this as a route into university with any confidence. But if there were a standardized system of college credit assessment, and every university agreed to recognize it on the same terms, we would already be well on our way to a model similar to CEGEP. Then, a student might attend college, and justifiably say to friends, family, and parents that it's the first step in a larger system of education. The stigma might not disappear entirely, but I think college would find acceptance by more people who currently aren't willing to consider that route.

The Teaching Institution

Even without a formal system that moves from colleges focused on teaching to universities focused on research, there's a natural distinction among universities in Canada. Some pitch themselves as primarily undergraduate schools whereas others position themselves as research centres. The institution devoted to undergraduate instruction is naturally motivated to focus on quality teaching and the classroom experience of its students. It may not even support a graduate program. The research institution, in contrast, is motivated to recruit professors for their success at publication, but with less attention paid to their ability as instructors. Additionally, the resources of the research university, and the time and attention of its faculty, may flow disproportionately into its graduate program. In both cases, the institutions will suggest they can have their cake and eat it too. The undergraduate universities will insist they house top scholars, just as the research universities will claim they offer the best instructors, but obviously there's a trade-off.

Various authorities have argued in the past, and with some justification, that most undergraduate students at the universities with the big reputations never benefit directly from the research conducted around them. They might do better at smaller liberal arts universities, such as Mount Allison in New Brunswick, or St. Francis Xavier in Nova Scotia — universities many students may not even be aware of. In many cases, it is no doubt true that students could benefit from education focused on the undergraduate level, but the gravitational force toward one standard of excellence throws this generalization into question. If enough top students choose the large institutions, regardless of the logic behind this choice, the standard of excellence travels with them, and it becomes a self-fulfilling trend. This is a shame, of course, because students don't win in this situation, and simply end up indirectly subsidizing research that doesn't benefit them.

Various Options

A great help to students would be the integration of colleges and universities into a properly coherent system of post-secondary education. By any name, or set of names, we have various institutions devoted to post-secondary education, but students can't easily distinguish what one does as opposed to another, and certainly can't move easily between them. Despite some ad hoc partnerships, students have no assurance of how their college diplomas will be received by a university admissions office, or how their transfer credits might be assessed. And despite some interesting "post-graduate" college programs pitched to university grads, there's very little standardization in terms of the nature or structure of such programs. As education lasts longer, and more and more students pursue post-secondary education at multiple institutions, they deserve a better road map.

It's also important to differentiate between undergraduate universities and research institutions, and to somehow get that point across to students, their parents, high-school teachers, and guidance counsellors. The recently published *Rae Review*, which examined the educational system in Ontario, made exactly this recommendation on a govern-mental level. The report recommended that governmental funding formulas and treatment of institutions should reflect their differing missions and characters. This is all well and good as a recom-mendation to government, but I think it's just as important to promote an awareness of this difference more widely. If the difference isn't made clear to students, and the adults who are advising them (or pushing them, or forcing them, as the case may be), then the gravitational force that wants to collapse all these distinctions will only do its work again.

I have other and more radical suggestions

regarding the realignment of the dominant institutions in higher education, and I'll get to those in a moment, but if you're reading this book before you commit yourself to one path or another, I urge you strongly to investigate all your options. Most of what's wrong with the system today isn't a distinct lack of options or appropriately personal paths, but a lack of awareness and respect for alternative choices. Far too many students within travelling distance of the larger institutions go there simply because they are "the best," but this concept is as flawed and inexact as the notion of universal success. If you still have time to think about what kind of educational experience you want, then take that opportunity while you can.

Break the Monopoly

This one is for all the career-minded folks out there. If your goal is to get out and work, and all you're looking for out of education is what you need to succeed in your career, then maybe this government-sanctioned monopoly over education isn't doing you that much good. So let's privatize! I'm really not kidding. Let the academics wring their hands about the evils of corporations and private industry in the classrooms. But as long as we're serious about differentiating the various functions of education, maybe it can work on a limited basis. Of course we don't want industry influencing education as it relates to liberal arts, natural sciences, or free inquiry. But when we're talking about directed vocational learning, that's a different story.

The Microsoft School of Computer Science

Okay, seriously, why not? I happen to hate corporate branding as much as the next guy, but if I wanted to learn computer science in a way that would give me a career in the sector, I'd be looking to learn it from a company that's generated careers. Big corporations are always trying to get their hooks into universities like this, and there's a continual tension relating to independence, academic freedom, and all kinds of things that the average student who just wants to work couldn't care less about. That's a problem because directed vocational learning has been folded into the same institutions that are trying to carry out research and pure inquiry. So separate them! If the academy wants independence, let it have it. And let students who just want jobs benefit from whatever private-sector partnerships can be arranged for them. But without extensive taxpayer support.

Industry has been spoiled by the degree of free service it receives from governments and from the education system. Back before central governments were so accommodating, any trade or guild that wanted to standardize and perpetuate their craft ran their own schools, or relied on apprenticeship. Maybe it's time to resurrect the idea. I don't doubt that in many industries and occupations, there's plenty of demand among students to learn from companies and industry leaders in their respective fields. So really it's just a matter of finding ways to get industry back at the table in a meaningful way, and get it to start paying more of the cost.

Independent Certification

As a more limited option, one that's used in many fields, the idea of professional certification is very important, and a growing trend. Professional guilds are not quite the force they once were, but associations and internal regulatory bodies are still at work in many fields. When those bodies administer standardized tests and establish internal standards for important certifications and qualifications, they have, in effect, reclaimed part of the responsibility for monitoring their respective professions. Many skilled and professional trades have bodies that regulate standards and qualifications in their fields — it happens in the practice of law and accounting, just as it occurs in welding and mechanics.

The major problem with these professional overseeing bodies, from my view, is that they are regarded only as a final control mechanism, rather than a real test of a particular candidate's quality. The standard is essentially one of qualified/unqualified, and then potential employers go back to judging you on the quality and origin of your degree. To an extent, this will always be true. We'll never get away from it entirely, but if we can cut away at least some of the false status attached to university (and specific universities), it could give rise to the sorts of niche education that would really benefit some students and some fields of employment. Remember Bob's School of Journalism? Yep, I'm on about that again.

What if these tests were so thorough and comprehensive that they could provide proof of anyone's abilities in a recognized way? What if anyone could walk in off the street and ask to be examined for qualification in a particular field? Of course it would still require years of education before anyone could pass the exam, but rather than require proof of the education separately, let the exam stand on its own. If I can pass, does it really matter where and how I learned what I know? If the test is good enough, it shouldn't. This principle could be applied to many professions, thus indirectly legitimizing something like Bob's School of Journalism. It really isn't such a foreign concept. That's how driving schools function — and lives depend on capable driving. It might also solve much of the long-standing problem of how to recognize foreign qualifications, providing entry to the Canadian job market for those who hold them.

Professional guilds and associations are good for industry, and they're good for education. They

> What if anyone could walk in off the street and ask to be examined for qualification in a particular field?

transfer at least a portion of the weight away from the degree, and if that can be encouraged — both in fields where associations already exist, and perhaps even where none exist — it could only be good for all concerned. Government incentives to establish and legitimize these associations would be a good investment in education, and a service to future students. If those associations could be encouraged to further legitimize learning and skills emerging from less traditional institutions, then so much the better.

Civil Service

Many nations in the world practise some form of mandatory civil service. This practice was originally rooted in traditions of compulsory military service, but where alternatives to the military were offered, the program inevitably grew toward greater and greater civil components. Canada has no such tradition, but it might be a shame we don't. Consider, for a moment, the merits of the system. Students often talk about spending a year planting trees or something similar, and some parents even approve of the idea, but then we all get caught up in the rhetoric of "not falling behind," or some other justification for going directly into post-secondary schooling. Our whole system, at the end of high school, is stacked against students who want to do anything different with their lives. There are seminars, counselling sessions, and organized tours of universities, but can anyone recall a session on how to spend a year working in the north, volunteering with disadvantaged kids, or even the stereotypical tree planting? Much as we allow the value of these experiences, and even admire the people who seek them out, it still seems countercultural to actually do it.

If we are streaming everyone directly into university before they're ready for it, and especially if we aren't prepared to make a general statement that they are adults in every sense when they get there, then maybe we need to find something else to do with these "kids" while they grow up. Some parents see the value of taking a year off to work or travel, and some don't, but most of the objections are rooted in what everyone else is doing. The fear of falling behind is all about what everyone else is up to. The fear of not returning to school is founded in what's "normal." If it were entirely typical to spend a year or two doing something else between high school and university, both those fears would be groundless. So how about we challenge the norm?

I propose that the Canadian government should institute between one and two years of mandatory civil service for every young adult, after high school. This would become a prerequisite to attending college or university. Various programs could be adopted to provide different options: social work in the community, environmental work in our very wide nation, certainly the choice of military service for those who want it. It could be an opportunity to experience new things, to meet new friends, to maybe travel and see more of Canada, and certainly to grow up a little. This labour should be paid, but it needn't pay very well. After all, it's more about the experience than anything else, right?

Remember the holding pen for a moment.

Remember the educational arms race fuelled by nothing so much as the fact that the workforce can't immediately absorb everyone after graduation. If you need to be somewhere, and need to be doing something, we've agreed that education is as good an activity as any other, except when you factor in the cost. Wouldn't it be great if, for a change, you could do something at least somewhat educational, and spend a couple of years figuring things out in a way that actually left you with a bit of money in your pockets rather than in debt? Would it be so terrible if, at the cost of a year or two, you had more time to get a bit of perspective before making irreparable choices about your future?

I can just imagine all the readers out there feeling betrayed right now. You all figured I was on your side, and I've just gone and proposed that you should all be forced to work for the government for a couple of years. Well, don't worry about it too much because I'm not in a position to make this happen anyway. But isn't there anything at all you wished you had the chance to try out? Aren't we all a little miffed that higher education seems to demand that we "grow up" in an awful hurry, long before we're treated like adults in any other meaningful way? Maybe it wouldn't be the worst thing in the world to slow it all down by just a year or two. Do something worthwhile, but under a lot less pressure.

CHAPTER EIGHT

GRASSROOTS CHANGE

Shaking Things Up

I hope, if you've made it this far in my book, I've successfully illustrated the point that the idea of university is up for debate. There are different understandings of what university is and does, and competing visions of what it could be and should be doing. University may not, in any fair sense, "belong" to a particular interest group, but it isn't unreasonable to promote or even fight for your vision of university. This happens all around us as various individuals and forces continually push for policies, programs, and initiatives based around their visions. You have just as much right to the institution as they do, so if you want to do something about it, that's just fine. In fact it's great, because it will probably make you a better, happier, more successful student.

I'm going to suggest a variety of things you can do that might advance your particular goals and priorities. If these specific ideas don't appeal to you, that's okay. You can always do your own thing, or else skip this part entirely. But I figure I owe you all some practical suggestions of ways you can not only get the most out of the system, but perhaps change it a little bit too. Some people just feel better if they can do something about the things they don't like.

If you make the effort to get what you want out of university, and if you go the extra mile to help other students get the same, you'll inevitably come into contact with people who feel the same way you do. That community of like-minded students can become the nucleus of something special. It might be what makes all the difference for you, and maybe for other people too. You can do a lot of good by fighting for what you want from your experience, and your investment.

Unofficial Classes

This one is mainly for the academics out there, but it might also appeal to the student radicals, and anyone interested in wholesale social reform. In an environment that's designed around selling education, there's nothing more radical than giving it away for free. For a working model of this idea, look at Anarchist U, a free education program that's run in Toronto.[1] You don't need to be an anarchist to appreciate the value of education. We all have things we would like to learn, and everyone has at least something to teach.

If you believe that education and university are supposed to be all about learning for its own sake, divorced from certification and careerism, then it doesn't really matter if you do or don't get credit for learning, right? Well, okay, let's back away from that idealism at least a little. Even the most committed academic usually acknowledges the need for some

professional recognition. Maybe it's a shame, but we all acknowledge it: frequently isn't about what you know, but what you can prove you know. So we still need the degree at the end of the road. But maybe you don't need a grade for absolutely everything you learn. Maybe you'd even appreciate the chance to learn something without the pressure of grading, and the fear of what it might do to your average. Maybe you'd like to do something so different that it doesn't fit into the formal curriculum at all. Maybe you even have something you'd be willing and able to teach. I hope you have something you can teach, actually, because it has to start somewhere.

I've talked about how professors are lifelong students and how anyone can be a teacher in the proper context. University students who learn this lesson early have a huge advantage over those still caught up in the absolute distinction between student and teacher. Peer-to-peer education breaks down this artificial barrier and forces people to confront the reality that learning is learning, whatever the source. Students around you have areas of expertise, just as your professors do. Perhaps their expertise isn't extensive enough to form the basis of an entire program, or even a full course, but surely just about anyone can teach a class or two, assuming they're willing. It's a pretty scary idea, but if you can muster the courage to start, maybe others will follow.

> Peer-to-peer education forces people to confront the reality that learning is learning, whatever the source.

In practical terms, the start-up required to offer a free class or two on a particular subject shouldn't be extensive. Find a space, find your audience, and tell them what you'd like to do. Then do it. If you can't bear all the responsibility of the project alone, you could begin by calling however many friends and like-minded people together that you can find, and host a general discussion around the topic. Maybe someone else will volunteer to go first. In any case, the key to this kind of plan, as with any other, is to start small and grow from there. No one builds an empire overnight, but if you get even a single course started, or a small series of one-shot classes, that should generate some attention.

Once things get rolling, you should definitely look to the larger university community for help. Get in touch with other students through whatever channels are available. If you need to recruit a little more content into your "curriculum," you might look to senior undergraduates, grad students (if you have them around), or even radical professors. If you can get a professor or two involved, you'll have something. If they all seem far too conventional and mired in "the system" to have any interest in what you're doing, then you need to go back to first principles, and remember that they're just like you except they've been at it decades longer. Maybe a lot of them are too busy and conservative and won't be interested in what you're doing, but there will still be an exception or two. A lot of student radicals and idealistic young academics end up staying in school for life, and not all of them forget their roots. Don't overlook campus media when it comes to advertising your activities. This sort of thing makes a good story.

Free universities have been done before and can be done again. You might find things get a little (or a lot) disorganized at times. You might even become a victim of your own success. If it does get off the ground, you'll find that all the same debates about priorities and goals may reoccur among the active base of participants you recruit. But still, the effort is worthwhile if only for the adventure of it, and for the sake of the people you'll meet. If you do get something up and running, please let me know. I promise if I'm ever in the area, I'll drop by for a class.

Clubs and Organizations

Just about everyone has something they are interested in doing that doesn't relate exactly to university. Everyone has a hobby. And I guarantee that among the many students around you, there are some who are into the same things you're into. That's what clubs and similar organizations are for. You don't have to think "chess club" if that's not what you're into. How about the "promoting fair trade and sweatshop-free purchasing" club? I've seen it, or at least something similar. So why not a club for whatever you're into?

You really only need to start a club when no one else is doing the same thing already. If there's already a group on the ground that's doing what you're into, or doing something really similar, then you are probably better off to get involved there. The problem with students just entering university is that year after year they imagine they are the first to ever have a really great idea. Now, maybe you actually are the first person to think of something really cool, but let's at least agree that the odds are against it. Some of the most inspired students get shut down and feel alienated in their first years at school because they have these really great ideas and wonder why everyone else isn't following them. Well, the fact is that most people would rather join something established, so unless your idea is genuinely unique, you're not going to get that immediate buy in. So look first at what already exists. If you're motivated, you'll find it incredibly easy to push for a new initiative or a personal idea, even in established groups, as long as you're willing to do most of the heavy lifting. If you are worried that existing groups will be resistant to new ideas, that's one of the advantages of student organizations. In an environment where the population of students is constantly turning over, the leadership of these groups changes

> You'll find it incredibly easy to push for a new initiative or a personal idea, even in established groups, as long as you're willing to do most of the heavy lifting.

on an annual basis, so there's always room for fresh blood and new ideas.

If getting involved with (or forming) a club or interest group is going to enrich your time at university, then go for it, but do it for the right reasons. Sometimes students imagine that involvement with a group is going to be such a big boost to their applications for graduate and professional school that careerism becomes the major motivation. That's flawed on two counts. First, it's a disservice to the group. No student group is well served by organizers who are primarily interested in using it as a career move. Second, it's simply not true that involvement with a student group is such a big deal to potential employers, or graduate or professional programs, that it's going to justify the time invested. If that's all you want from the experience, you'd be better off just focusing the extra time on your studies.

For a lot of students, clubs and campus groups are just a way to make some friends and meet like-minded people. If that's what you're looking for, then full speed ahead. University can be a lonely and anonymous place until you've met some people you have something in common with, so clubs are a good place to start. But beyond that, there's another level at which these groups can help you get down to the things that are important to your life. It isn't just about making university more bearable, or more profitable, it's about making university part of what's meaningful in the larger world. Some students never feel that need at all. For others, it's a gaping hole until it's filled.

Out in the Community

Some of the best groups for students who are looking for a more relevant experience from university are the ones that get you out into the community. It can be as simple as a campus group that takes students out to volunteer together with an existing community organization, or as complex as a whole initiative run entirely by students, though generally in partnership with an external organization. The benefit to partnering with community groups is that they provide training, stability, organization, and legitimacy. University students are in demand by all kinds of organizations that tend to assume students are intelligent and responsible. You may not feel like it sometimes, but they assume you are anyway.

There are student groups that run literacy programs and mentor at-risk youth. There are groups

that work with shelters and the homeless. Levels of commitment vary depending on the complexity of the work. It doesn't take much training to collect for the local food bank, but you've obviously got to get proper training before you walk into a shelter for abused women. Some of this isn't easy work; in fact, it's the kind of thing that can send first-timers into uncontrollable crying fits when they get home. But this work is also real, and it can be the defining experience that makes university real by extension.

Working with community groups is the exception to my do-it-yourself rule. I strongly encourage students who want to work in the community to get involved with existing student groups that are doing it. If there really isn't anything going on in the area that interests you, then you might consider taking the initiative to get a program off the ground. But be aware that it's a huge undertaking, especially in terms of the more specialized stuff, which requires training and expertise. Look to the university administration (Office of Student Affairs or similar) for help, look to your students' union or administrative council, and then talk to potential community partners. The upside of people assuming you're intelligent and responsible is that they'll let you in the door easily; the downside is that you've got to live up to the expectation, and do the work. If you want to work with vulnerable people, you assume a pretty huge obligation to get it right.

Industry Outreach

Not everything you do with campus groups needs to be altruistic. If you're looking for real-world experience and contacts for purely career-driven reasons, that's okay too. Lots of students are looking for some way to make their education relevant to their future careers, and the companies and industries that might provide those careers are interested in getting in touch with good students. Key word there is, of course, "good" students. If you're looking for more professional opportunities and contacts, that's great, but be professional in return. If you still expect your future employer to beat down the door to get to you, just look at the size of your classes and think again. Program-based clubs and student groups formed around career goals can provide an important link between university and that outside world.

I've mentioned mentorship programs as one popular way to bring the working world more closely in touch with university students. It takes a while to get a good mentorship program rolling, so if one exists for your area, then definitely take advantage of it. Ask your professors about opportunities, and poke around in any relevant clubs and student groups. If you find there isn't a program for you, it could be another do-it-yourself opportunity — those are still often the best kind. You gain so much more from making something happen than when someone simply hands it to you. It's a big task, don't get me wrong, but if you want to give it a shot, get in touch with whoever is responsible for alumni relations.

There are many other potential events for a student group interested in a particular industry or career. Job fairs are always popular, networking events, trips to local businesses in relevant areas, guest speakers, etc. Invent awards to give to local leaders in your field. Nothing draws in interest like an award to win. Present the award(s) at a year-end event of some sort, and it might net you some popular guests of honour. Of course it takes student support to make a group like this work, but if you see the demand, then move to fill it. Please though, don't try to reinvent the wheel and expect everyone else to buy your new wheel. If there's an existing group, you'll almost always do better working with them. If you have energy to give and time to invest, you can make the group your own. There is simply never too much, or even enough, good leadership. And it never hurts to arrive with good ideas.

Participating in Governance

This book, and my entire approach to university, is founded on the premise that students are more empowered when they understand their environment, and the institution around them. Sometimes, however, understanding just isn't enough. If you want to take the next step, and take some control over the system, there are many opportunities to do that. There's no one right reason to get involved with university governance and politics. Some students get involved because they are staunchly anti-establishment, while others are very dedicated to working with the system. The only basic requirement is to care about your experience at university, and hopefully have at least some willingness to take responsibility for other students' experiences as well.

There are several ways to get involved with

university governance. The most obvious is to work on a purely student level with your students' union, council, or whatever you have. Often there are varying levels to choose from, so you can start small, if you wish, with a college council or residence group, before moving into the big leagues. Of course the best thing is to start with whatever group or role relates to the things you care about. This might take a bit of research, but it isn't as intimidating as it sounds. Most of us have at least a general sense of the people who seem to know what's going on. So ask around. It's as simple as saying, "I care about this, who's doing something about that?" Eventually you will get pointed at the right person. And it goes from there.

Student groups inevitably work with the administration to get things done. The nature of that relationship varies considerably from case to case. At extremes of the spectrum, you may find the student group that represents you is sometimes hard to even distinguish from the administration, or else you may find that it gets into violent clashes with campus security. Only you can decide what sort of environment makes you the most comfortable, but remember that any group that includes you as a member has an obligation to at least take your views into account. If you aren't happy with the way it's conducting itself, you can get involved anyway, and do what you can to change it.

> Decision making should include all the stakeholders, which means administration, staff, faculty, and of course students.

In addition to the formal sorts of student organizations that work with university administration, the university itself will have a governance structure that includes students at many levels.

There's this fabulous concept out there that decision making should include all the stakeholders in the institution, which means administration, staff, faculty, and of course students. Believe me when I say that the student voice in the process can be incredibly important and influential, or it can be marginalized and included only in a token way. The tone of student involvement depends somewhat on the attitude of the administration, but also heavily on the students themselves. Sometimes the best students — with the will to be involved and the skills to really contribute — are turned away from these opportunities because they don't see them as meaningful. All I can say is that participation in university governance is what you make of it, but the potential, at least, is very real. The philosophical commitment to student involvement will get you a seat at the table where decisions are made. How much influence you have over those decisions depends on your ability to confront the same problems faced daily by university administrators, and to present a student perspective that's both progressive and constructive.

Sometimes the student representation within university governance will be drawn from existing student groups. Other times there might be independent positions. Again, the best way to figure out what's going on in this area is to track down the people in the know, and just ask them. Involved students are a mixed group just like anyone, and you might find a few jerks, but mostly you'll find people who will give you the whole big picture over a cup of coffee. I won't lie to you — university and student politics are definitely *politics*. It can get nasty at times. But when you approach it for the first time as

an outsider, you'll find most people you talk with are more than happy to draw you in and supply you with an endless amount of information and opinions. What you do with the information, and how far you take it, is up to you.

A lot of the opportunities to be involved with representative student groups and university governance require getting elected. Obviously that isn't everyone's style, which is a shame because some of the best people and potential representatives won't go into an election to save their own lives. The good news is there are usually quite a few ways to get involved, even without facing a general election. Some of the elections that do happen are often so quiet and minimal that if you have any stomach for it at all, you don't risk much by giving it a shot. Often even when you take a shot at some position and lose, involved students will notice and encourage you toward other opportunities to influence things that you care about.

More than anything else I've discussed, student and university governance is about playing the game rather than trying to "win." When you participate in something so much bigger than one person's efforts, you must accept, from the start, that your ability to create wholesale change is limited. You'll grapple with many big-picture issues, and may have to be satisfied with small steps and minor improvements, a lot of the time. But for those people who just need to do something and claim a bit of control over the things they don't like, this can be a great way to humanize university.

And yes. It looks good on a resumé. But like everything else, it also isn't worth so much that you'd want to do it just for the credit you'll receive. It's far better to get involved with something you care about so you can get credit for it and do something interesting at the same time.

Asking the Big Questions

The last and most basic thing you can do is to ask questions. It's also the most radical thing possible because it's the starting point of all change. You'll be confronted with plenty of difficult questions in the course of your studies. You may also find that the people you meet at university will provoke other questions, entirely unrelated to your formal education. If you are serious about school at all, your brain is guaranteed to get a workout while you're there, but there's no guarantee it will be working on the problems that are most important to you. In fact there's a real danger that university will keep you so busy thinking about everything else, you never have the energy to question university itself.

Why are you at school? What are you trying to accomplish? What do you value in life? These aren't idle questions, and they certainly don't belong solely to philosophers. In fact it's entirely possible to study philosophy in university and still avoid asking these important personal questions. The endless treadmill of course enrollment, and assignments, exams, grades, and eventual graduation conspires to keep students from thinking about the questions that matter. It creates a comforting perception of progress and achievement. The constant milestones and the undeniable evidence of "getting somewhere" stops students from asking where they're going, or why they started in that direction in the first place. And that's sad.

What I've tried to do, with this book, is to generate thought around these questions. Because I'm addressing many people at once, I've had to categorize. Of course it isn't really as simple as five types of people with similar motivations and goals. The framework is useful, but it's also limited. As always I encourage you: take from this book what you can use, and leave what you can't. But ask the questions. And if you decide there's something you want from university and education, and if I haven't offered any useful tips for how to get it, then go after it anyway as best you can. Life's like

> Talk to the students around you. Ask them why they are there. Talk to faculty whenever you get a chance. Ask them why they are there.

that, after all, and you can't always have a guide.

Talk to the students around you. Ask them why they are there. Talk to faculty whenever you get a chance. Ask them why they are there. Please don't assume your professors know what they are doing with their lives just because they have jobs, kids, and mortgages. You'll be missing half the substance of their conversation if you assume they've got easy answers. Ask them what kind of university they believe in. Take some notes. Pretty soon you'll be more qualified to give advice to students and to talk about the big problems than most so-called experts. Write to me and let me know if you discover anything new. Write a rebuttal to this book if you want, and tell me I'm full of shit. If I generate enough thought on this subject to motivate a rebuttal, I'll be thrilled. I don't have all the answers. I've just got some of the most important questions. Now so do you.

Pass along the tough questions. It's dangerous to get comfortable with all your assumptions when you're investing thousands upon thousands of dollars and years of your life in something. Even if you're pretty sure you're on the right track and feel good about things, you should still revisit the questions once in a while. And if you can make the students around you just a little bit uncomfortable with their assumptions, it's probably the best thing you could do for them. Get involved with your school's orientation activities, and talk with frosh when they show up. Ask them why they've come to university. Make them confront the same issues. Get them early when they have the most time possible to think about these things, and maybe they'll have some good answers by the time they are done, at least.

Use this book or don't use this book. I hope it's a useful aid that gets you thinking, with some fun facts about university, so that when you talk about it you can sound smart. I hope I've helped in your understanding of the institution and how it operates. But in any case, don't imagine this book, or any other, is sufficient by itself to help you get what you want. The most terrible and liberating part about "growing up" (in case you're waiting for that) is when you realize that everyone else still feels just as confused as you do. So why in the world would you blindly trust anyone else to make decisions for you? You can learn a lot from other people, who may be more experienced than you, but they can't tell you what you want from life, or what will make you happy. They can only tell you how to best realize your goals once you know what they are, as I've tried to do.

You're reading a book by a thirty-one-year-old guy who left high school at nineteen, and went to work at a Tim Hortons. I washed floors, bussed tables, did a bit of construction work, made lattes, sold computers, and at one point even pulled a rickshaw for a living. I bummed around for eight years, then began university and went to work for my students' union. Now I serve as a director on the board of a national not-for-profit corporation, and I'll be attending law school. If I qualify as an expert on this subject, that's the best evidence possible that nothing at all is standardized in life, or in university, and no one is qualified to answer questions about your life but you. It's a little scary, maybe, but also comforting to know there's at least one subject on which you can never be contradicted. Decide what you want from university and go for it, or else get out while you can, and return when you're ready. And cross the next bridge when you get there.

---

1 You can find the website for Anarchist U at www.anarchistu.org, current as of the publication date of this book. In their FAQ, they describe themselves as follows: "The Anarchist U is a volunteer-run collective which organizes a variety of courses on arts and sciences. Most courses run for ten weeks, and meet once a week; there are no admission fees. The Anarchist U follows the tradition of free schools in that it is open, non-hierarchic, and questions the roles of teachers and students."

I am extremely grateful and indebted to many people for the wonderful time I had as an undergraduate student, and that experience is impossible to separate from the substance of this book. The University of Toronto Scarborough was the proving ground for this material. I'd like to thank all the students there for allowing me to serve three years as their representative, and staff and faculty for many candid conversations that contributed so much to my understanding of university. It was never my plan to attend UTSC in the first place, but the community made the experience something special, and there's nowhere else I would sooner have been.

Even a partial list of friends and colleagues who contributed especially will be long, but I'd like to recognize: Jon Agg, Sheraz Arshad, Asma Bala, Dan Bandurka, Guy Brisebois, Melissa Calder, Nick Cheng, Curtis Cole, Lendyl D'Souza, Mathieu Dagonas, Teressa Dawson, Drew Dudley, Vinitha Gengatharan, Bill Gough, Allan Grant, Brian Harrington, Paul Hunter, Janis Jones, Jemy Joseph, Leah Ko, Rashelle Litchmore, Travis Lunau, Don MacMillan, Ron Manzer, Kim McLean, Mike

Morrow, Tom Nowers, Kevin Ramcharan, Gillian Reiss, Ruthie Szamosi, Virata Thaivasigamony, Chris Van Abbema, Susie Vavrusa, Preet Virdi, Adam Watson, and Rob Wulkan.

As traditional as it is to thank one's family, I'd like to acknowledge a special debt to my parents who supported my education in the best way possible — by leaving me alone and allowing me to wait until I was ready. Without that support, I am absolutely certain none of this would be possible.

ECW PRESS has been wonderful to me and I owe thanks to the entire office, in particular David Caron and Jack David. It's an honour to be associated with such a Canadian literary tradition. My editor, Emily Schultz, has contributed immeasurably to the final product of this book, and I'm especially grateful for her excellent work.

Finally, I'd like to thank Russell Brown. He has been that one special professor every student should be so lucky to discover — an enduring influence, a remarkable champion, and more, a good friend.

REFERENCES

"Bankruptcy and Insolvency Act." In *Revised Statutes of Canada*, 1985, chapter B-3. Ottawa: Queen's Printer, 1985.

Ben-Ishai, Stephanie. "One Paradox of the Bankruptcy Fresh Start: Government Student Loans." In *Annual Review of Insolvency Law 2005*, edited by Janis P. Sarra. Toronto: Thomson Carswell, 2006.

"Canada Student Loans Act." In *Revised Statutes of Canada*, 1985, chapter S-23. Ottawa: Queen's Printer, 1985.

"Canada Post Corporation Act." In *Revised Statutes of Canada*, 1985, chapter C-10. Ottawa: Queen's Printer, 1985.

Coulter, Rebecca Priegert, and Ivor F. Goodson. *Rethinking Vocationalism: whose work/life is it?* Toronto: Our Schools/Our Selves Education Foundation, 1993.

Dickson, Tom. *Mass Media Education in Transition: Preparing for the 21st Century.* New Jersey: Lawrence Erlbaum Associates, 2000.

Finnie, Ross. "A Matter of Discipline: Early Career Outcomes of Recent Canadian University Graduates." In *Renovating the Ivory Tower: Canadian Universities and the Knowledge Economy*, edited by David Laidler, 169-214. Ottawa: C.D. Howe Institute, 2002.

Gidney, R.D. *From Hope to Harris: The Reshaping of Ontario's Schools.* Toronto: University of Toronto Press, 1999.

Leslie, Larry, and Paul Brinkman. *The Economic Value of Higher Education.* New York: Collier, 1988.

Looker, E. Dianne. "Interconnected Transitions and Their Costs: Gender and Urban/Rural

Differences in the Transitions to Work." In *Transitions: Schooling and Employment in Canada*, edited by Paul Anisef and Paul Axelrod, 43-64. Toronto: Thompson Educational Publishing, 1993.

Millar v. Smith and Co. [1925] 3 Dominion Law Reports 267, Saskatchewan Court of Appeal.

Ontario Ministry of Education and Training. *Ontario Secondary Schools, Grades 9–12: Program and Diploma Requirements*. Toronto: Queen's Printer for Ontario, 1999. Also available at http://www.edu.gov.on.ca/eng/document/curricul/secondary/oss/oss.pdf.

"Post Secondary Education and Excellence Act, 2000." In *Statutes of Ontario*, 2000, chapter 36. Toronto: Queen's Printer for Ontario, 2000.

Rathje, Kelly Ann, and J.C. Herbert Emery. "Returns to University Education in Canada Using New Estimates of Program Costs." In *Renovating the Ivory Tower: Canadian Universities and the Knowledge Economy*, edited by David Laidler, 241-64. Ottawa: C.D. Howe Institute, 2002.

Stamp, Robert M. *Ontario Secondary School Program Innovations and Student Retention Rates: 1920s-1970s*. Toronto: Queen's Printer for Ontario, 1988.

Vaillancourt, François, and Sandrine Bourdeau-Primeau. "The Returns to University Education in Canada, 1990 and 1995." In *Renovating the Ivory Tower: Canadian Universities and the Knowledge Economy*, edited by David Laidler, 215-40. Ottawa: C.D. Howe Institute, 2002.

JEFF RYBAK graduated in 2006 from the University of Toronto Scarborough, where he served in the students' union as Vice-President Academics and within campus governance as Chair of the Academic Committee. He spent many hours counselling students on how to deal with all aspects of university, and was responsible for the production of several resources for students, including three editions of the campus *Anti-Calendar*. Jeff is currently a director on the board of the Canadian Internet Registration Authority (CIRA), and is pursuing a law degree at the University of Toronto.

www.JeffRybak.ca

EVAN MUNDAY's work has appeared in *This Magazine, Broken Pencil, Shameless Magazine, Alternatives Journal, Matrix,* and other publications. He produces *The Amazing Challengers of Unknown Mystery*, a comic book chronicling the lives of Waterloo, Ontario's greatest superheroes. He lives in Toronto.